PRACTICAL MOON MAGIC

Leaping Hare Press

PRACTICAL MOON MAGIC

KATIE HUANG
Founder of LOVE BY LUNA

Illustrated by **Amirah Sheikh**

CONTENTS

INTRODUCTION

Welcome to *Practical Moon Magic*, your gateway to understanding and harnessing the enchanting power of the moon. Whether you're just beginning to explore the world of moon magic or seeking to deepen an existing connection, this book is designed to guide you through each phase of the lunar cycle and show you how to integrate this ancient wisdom into your modern life.

The moon, with its constant changes from new to full, serves as a beautiful metaphor for our own lives. Just like the moon, we are constantly evolving, growing, and transforming. As a visible and essential part of our existence, the moon mirrors our own cycles of change, reminding us that every phase we go through has its unique beauty and purpose. This is one reason the moon has always been one of my favorite celestial bodies; it's a constant companion in the sky, reflecting our own light back to us, and reminding us that change is not only natural but also necessary for growth.

In these pages, you'll discover the profound influence the moon has on our lives, uncovering the unique energies of each lunar phase and learning how to harness them through tools, rituals, and practices. You'll also delve into the moon's role in astrology as it moves through each zodiac sign, revealing how this transition affects our emotional landscape. From setting powerful intentions with the new moon to letting go with the full moon, this guide provides practices that make it easy to tap into the moon's energies. No matter the phase, you'll find ways to make the moon's power work for you.

CHAPTER

1

THE MAGIC OF THE MOON

The moon is magical for many reasons, but to fully appreciate and understand its power, we must first observe it.

If you look up at the night sky, you'll notice it's never the same from one evening to the next. The moon's phases vividly demonstrate life's constant flux—growing from a sliver of light to full brilliance, then fading back into darkness. These endless transformations reflect a fundamental truth in the human experience: change is the only constant.

Change isn't always easy to embrace. When we face the unknown, an overwhelming amount of "what ifs" swirl in our heads. What if something bad happens? What if I fail? What if this decision isn't the right one? Contemplating every potential mishap can leave us frozen in fear. So, what do we do? We cling to the comfort of what we know. We make excuses, pass on opportunities, and stick to the same routines.

If these feelings echo your own experiences, you aren't alone. The moon is a great teacher when it comes to embracing change. In this chapter, we'll dive into the transformative power of the moon, exploring how its cycles help us navigate transitions and encourage personal growth. We'll also look at how it influences our bodies, moods, and surroundings, offering practical ways to work with its energy to bring about positive shifts in our lives.

HOW THE MOON HAS HELPED ME

One of the greatest gifts of working with the moon is its ability to guide us through the ever-changing seasons and chapters of our lives. But, to access this energy, we must be willing to embrace change. The truth is, many of us resist change, often without even realizing it, because it's part of our natural instinct to avoid the unknown. Uncertainty can be scary, and staying in our comfort zone feels safer. However, I've learned through my own experiences that when we lean into those shifts and learn to flow with them, they almost always lead us toward something better, even if it doesn't seem that way at first.

To illustrate this, I want to share a quick personal story. When I founded Love By Luna, my astrology-inspired lifestyle brand, in 2015, I managed all our social media content by myself for the first four years. It wasn't long before the endless cycle of creating, scheduling, and posting led to burnout. I knew that hiring help could free up my time to focus on other areas of the business, but the idea of giving up creative control was daunting, so I stuck to doing everything myself.

Unsurprisingly, this resistance eventually caught up to me. After months of nonstop content creation, I hit a wall of total exhaustion. I felt uninspired and disconnected from the business I had built. It wasn't until I reached this low point that I realized something had to change. Ironically, when I finally embraced the idea of letting go, things started to fall into place almost magically. I hired a social media assistant who not only understood our branding but also brought fresh ideas that revitalized our content. This allowed me to refocus on other important areas of my business and take much-needed time to recharge. With this shift, both my energy and the business began to thrive again.

Looking back, I can see that my fears about giving up control were unfounded. Embracing change opened doors I hadn't expected and proved that my initial doubts were merely obstacles I'd created. This experience taught me that change, while scary, can be the catalyst for growth and new opportunities. Sometimes the universe pushes us to level up. When we allow it, we can discover just how much good can come from embracing the unknown.

So, I encourage you to stay open to change. When the fear of the unknown creeps in, remember that it might just be the prelude to an incredible new chapter. The moon teaches us this lesson time and again—its constant cycle of renewal shows us the power of staying fluid and evolving with each phase of our journey. Just like the moon, we are meant to shift, grow, and embrace each day as a stepping stone to something greater.

HOW THE MOON CAN HELP YOU

At this point, you might be wondering, "I get that the moon represents change, but how can something so distant impact my everyday life?" Surprisingly, the moon is not some far-off cosmic body that we only gaze at from time to time. Its influence is woven into many aspects of our daily lives. When you begin to work with the moon's cycles, you can live more in tune with the present moment. The moon is a guide for understanding the ebb and flow of energy, both in the world around us and within ourselves. By tuning into its phases, you can gain a better sense of when to push forward, when to slow down and when to simply take stock of where you are.

Each phase of the moon offers a distinct energy that reflects our own cycles of growth and rest. For example, during the waxing phase, the moon's light increases, signaling a time to initiate new projects and set intentions. You might notice a natural rise in your energy levels during this time, making it ideal for pursuing goals and taking decisive action. As the moon wanes and its light dims, you may find yourself craving rest or reflection. This is your cue to let go of what's no longer serving you—whether it's old habits, unfinished tasks, or mental clutter. By paying attention to the moon's subtle shifts, you can begin to align your actions with the natural flow of energy around you, creating greater harmony and balance in your life.

Historically, the moon has long been used to track time—marking the seasons, harvests, and significant life events. Our ancestors looked to the moon to navigate their days and prepare for the future. Similarly, we can use the lunar cycle as a tool for measuring our own progress. Checking in with the moon gives you a moment to pause and evaluate your journey. Are you moving toward your goals, or is it time to reassess your path? By regularly engaging with the moon's phases, you create space for self-reflection, fostering deeper personal growth and more intentional living.

Now that you've seen how the moon's cycles can guide and support you, let's explore the many ways it shapes our daily lives.

HOW THE MOON SHAPES OUR LIVES

The moon's influence extends far beyond the visual and metaphorical; it has tangible effects on our physical, emotional, and psychological states, reinforcing its role as a source of wisdom. In this exploration, we'll uncover the broader impacts of the moon and how they pertain to these aspects of our lives.

PHYSICAL INFLUENCES

The moon governs the tides, its gravitational pull regulating the vast oceans. More subtly, it affects the water within our own bodies. Its influence can also be seen in agricultural patterns. Farmers have long planted, pruned, and harvested according to the lunar cycle, observing that seeds tend to absorb more water during the full moon (due to the moon's gravitational pull on soil moisture), enhancing their growth.

When it comes to our bodies, historical beliefs and some modern studies suggest synchronization between the menstrual cycle and lunar phases, with peak fertility potentially coinciding with the full moon when bioluminescence is brightest. Some traditions propose that the body's capacity for healing, detoxification, and rejuvenation is tied to the moon's phases. Activities like starting a new diet, detox, or exercise regimen are often aligned with specific lunar phases to maximize effectiveness. For example, the waxing moon is seen as beneficial for starting new health initiatives, while the waning moon is often chosen for detoxification processes.

EMOTIONAL AND PSYCHOLOGICAL INFLUENCES

The moon has long been believed to exert psychological effects on humans, a phenomenon often reflected in cultural stories, folklore, and divinatory practices such as astrology. Many attribute fluctuations in mood and behavior to the lunar cycle, particularly during the full moon when increases in restlessness, insomnia, and emotional intensity are commonly reported. Some theories suggest that the full moon's light may disrupt sleep, leading to sleep deprivation that affects mood and cognitive function. Furthermore, the moon's phases are thought to influence human psychology symbolically—new moons are associated with new beginnings and setting intentions, while full moons are seen as times for release and reflection. While scientific evidence on lunar effects remains mixed, the persistent cultural beliefs underline a deep psychological connection between humans and the lunar cycle.

As you begin to observe the moon and its cycles, you may notice patterns in your own life and tune into how the moon's energy might be influencing your personal and professional activities. It's a tool that requires no special equipment—just a willingness to pay attention to the night sky and perhaps maintain a simple moon diary.

In the next chapter, we'll dive deeper into an overview of the lunar cycle, outlining its distinct phases and the unique energy each one brings.

CHAPTER

2

THE MOON AND ITS PHASES

Isn't it reassuring to know that each night, the moon provides a fresh perspective, a new energy to tap into? It's like the universe has already reserved a space for us to explore and expand our awareness. Whether it's the hectic weekdays or the quiet evenings, the moon's phases invite us to reflect on different aspects of our lives, offering us the chance to realign our goals and track our progress. That said, understanding the detailed workings of the lunar cycle is key to leveraging the moon's power. By tuning in to the moon's movement, we can stay connected to our intentions and bring more clarity to our daily lives.

THE LUNAR CYCLE

The lunar cycle, also known as a lunation, spans approximately twenty-nine and a half days and represents the period during which the moon completes a full orbit around the Earth. This cycle begins with the new moon, when the moon is positioned between the Earth and the sun, rendering it invisible from our perspective. As the moon orbits Earth, it gradually becomes more visible, moving through phases of waxing (growing) until it reaches the full moon, when it is fully illuminated. After the full moon, the moon enters the waning (decreasing) phase, during which its visible portion diminishes until it cycles back to the new moon.

As the moon journeys through its different phases, it brings distinct energies and opportunities for transformation. Each phase carries its own unique influence, offering moments for reflection, intention-setting, and action.

There are several ways to observe and engage with the moon's phases:

THE EIGHT-PHASE SYSTEM:

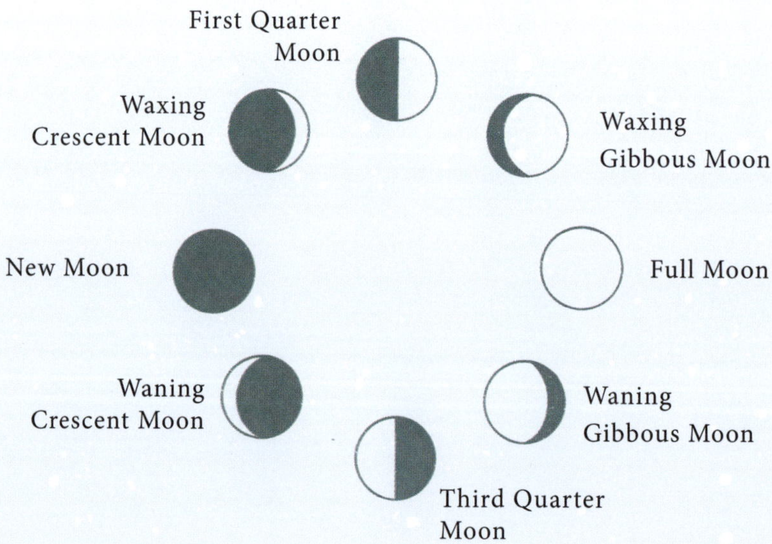

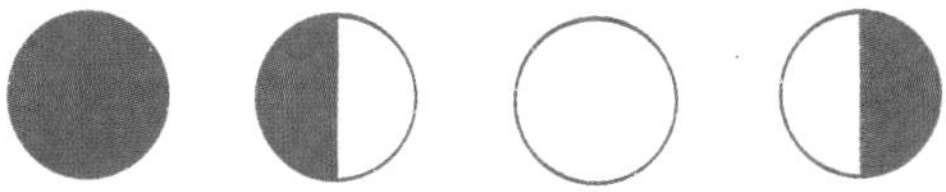

THE FOUR-PHASE SYSTEM:

NEW MOON, WAXING MOON, FULL MOON, WANING MOON

The main difference between this system and the eight-phase system is that it emphasizes broader themes of growth and release, offering a more streamlined understanding of lunar influences. By consolidating multiple phases into simply waxing moon and waning moon, this approach encourages individuals to focus on the overarching cycles of expansion and contraction, rather than the subtle distinctions of each phase.

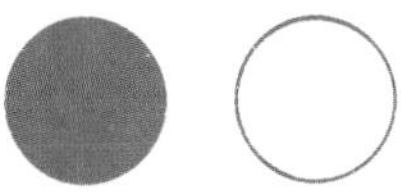

THE TWO-PHASE SYSTEM:

NEW MOON, FULL MOON

This simplified system focuses exclusively on the two pivotal points of the lunar cycle: the new moon and the full moon. By concentrating attention to these key moments, it is particularly beneficial for beginners or for those seeking to integrate lunar practices into a busy lifestyle.

Ultimately, the choice of which lunar phases to celebrate or which system to follow is entirely up to you. For the purposes of this book, we will explore the eight-phase system as it offers the most depth, and I wouldn't want you to miss out on all the juicy details and subtle nuances of each phase! However, it's perfectly okay to simplify your practice when life gets hectic. I often alternate between the four-phase and two-phase systems depending on my schedule and needs at the time. The important thing is to find a balance that works for you.

TRACKING THE MOON'S PHASES

Now that you have a general understanding of the energy associated with each lunar phase, you can begin to align your activities by tracking the moon's movements. A simple way to do this is to know how long each phase lasts. For instance, each phase of the moon—new moon, first quarter, full moon, and third quarter—takes about seven days. So, if you know when one phase begins, you can roughly count the days until the next one.

Here's a quick breakdown:

New Moon to First Quarter | ~ SEVEN DAYS

First Quarter to Full Moon | ~ SEVEN DAYS

Full Moon to Third Quarter | ~ SEVEN DAYS

Third Quarter to New Moon | ~ SEVEN DAYS

Following this basic cycle allows you to stay attuned to the moon's energy, even without a detailed calendar.

If you prefer something more precise, a lunar calendar is a great tool. There are many websites and apps that provide detailed lunar calendars tailored to your location, often including extra information like eclipses and other celestial events. If you like a more traditional approach, printed lunar calendars are also available and make a beautiful addition to your space. Having a physical calendar lets you see the whole year at a glance, which is incredibly helpful for planning ahead.

Whether you go digital or stick with a physical calendar, choose the option that best fits your lifestyle. Once you have your calendar ready, you'll be set to create a solid schedule for your moon-based practices and rituals.

CHAPTER 3

TOOLS OF MOON MAGIC

When it comes to working with the moon, magic is pretty much everywhere. There is an abundance of tools and correspondences that can enhance your connection to lunar energies, making your rituals and practices more powerful and effective. From the day of the week you choose to perform a ritual, to the color of the candle you light, every element plays a crucial role in helping you tap into the power of the moon. This chapter will explore these various tools and guide you on how to integrate them into your practices, allowing you to tailor your rituals for better alignment with your intentions.

UNDERSTANDING LUNAR CORRESPONDENCES

Lunar correspondences refer to the symbolic associations between the moon and various elements, such as days of the week, colors, flowers, herbs, deities, and crystals. These correspondences resonate with the moon's phases, helping to draw specific energies into your rituals and daily practices.

I like to think of correspondences as optional spices in a recipe—just as the right seasoning can enhance a dish, using certain correspondences can strengthen your intentions. If specific elements resonate with you, feel free to incorporate them into your rituals. However, be mindful not to overwhelm your practice with too many correspondences, as this can diminish your focus. The success of your ritual lies not in the number of elements included, but in how intentional you are in using them. A simple spell, executed with clarity and intent, can be just as powerful—if not more so—than one with a complex setup. The key is to approach your practice with purpose and balance, ensuring that each element enhances your intention rather than diluting it.

Ultimately, follow your intuition and choose what feels right for you. Now, let's delve into some of these correspondences to understand how they can enhance your connection with the moon.

DAYS OF THE WEEK

In astrology, each day of the week is connected to a planet, bringing distinct energies. Understanding these planetary influences allows you to align your actions and rituals with cosmic energies, optimizing their effectiveness.

SUNDAY **Sun**	Ruled by the sun, Sunday is perfect for personal power, success, and vitality. Focus on self-improvement, health, and achieving personal goals.
MONDAY **Moon**	Aligned with the moon, Monday is the best day for practices involving emotional well-being and psychic development. Use this day to set new intentions.
TUESDAY **Mars**	Mars brings energy, action, and assertiveness on Tuesday. It's a great day for courage, tackling difficult projects, and resolving conflicts.
WEDNESDAY **Mercury**	Mercury's influence makes Wednesday ideal for communication, learning, and commerce. It's the perfect day for studying, writing, and intellectual pursuits.
THURSDAY **Jupiter**	Thursday is ruled by Jupiter and supports expansion, growth, and luck. It's considered the best day for manifestation and working on financial success.
FRIDAY **Venus**	Venus brings love, beauty, and relationships to the forefront on Friday. Use this day for love spells, nurturing friendships, and artistic endeavors.
SATURDAY **Saturn**	Saturday is best for discipline, structure, and clearing obstacles. It's an ideal day for ending what no longer serves you and setting long-term goals.

THE WATER ELEMENT

Water is fluid, adaptable, and deeply connected to our emotions and subconscious. When you work with water, you tap into an element that embodies purification, intuition, and emotional depth. Consider how a calm lake reflects everything around it—water helps us see our own reflections and dive deeper into our feelings. This makes it perfect for connecting with the moon, which governs our inner worlds and emotions. Using water in your rituals can enhance your intuition, cleanse your spirit, and help you explore the mysterious, introspective qualities that the moon represents.

Moon Water

Create moon water by placing a jar of filtered water outside in the light of the moon. This water can then be used in spells, to cleanse crystals, or to anoint yourself during rituals, infusing your practice with lunar energy. You can also drink it, add it to recipes (use it as water for boiling pasta or as part of a soup base), or use it in a humidifier in your room. The possibilities are endless, so get creative!

Bath Rituals

Take a ritual bath during the new or full moon. As you soak, focus on cleansing yourself of negativity while drawing in the moon's instrospective and calming energies.

Scrying

Use a bowl of water for scrying during moon rituals. Gaze into the water's surface by moonlight to receive messages and insights from your subconscious and the lunar energies.

Meditation by Water

Meditate near a natural water source, like a river, or ocean, especially during the moonlit night. The rhythmic sound of the water can help you align with the moon's cycles and deepen intuitive insights.

Reflective Journaling

Perform reflective journaling near water. Write down your intentions, emotions, and any insights you gain while connecting with the water's tranquil energy, allowing the moon to guide your reflections.

Stay Hydrated

Charge a glass of filtered water under the moonlight and drink it with intention, focusing on internalizing the moon's energy. This practice can enhance your intuition and emotional clarity.

COLOR MAGIC

Color magic is a form of practice that uses the energy and symbolism of colors to enhance and direct magical workings. Each color carries unique properties and associations, making them powerful tools in rituals, spells, and everyday life. By intentionally incorporating specific colors into your magical practice, you can amplify your intentions to reach your desired outcomes.

Various ways to incorporate color magic include:

Candles | Choose candle colors that correspond to your intentions for spells and rituals.

Clothing and Accessories | Wear colors that align with your goals or emotional needs for the day.

Altar Decorations | Decorate your altar with colored cloths, crystals, and objects that match your magical focus.

Visualization | Meditate and visualize the color associated with your intention enveloping you or your desired outcome.

LUNAR COLORS

Silver, white, and blue are deeply connected to lunar energy and can be incorporated into your rituals through altar decorations or clothing.

SILVER Reflecting the moon's surface, silver enhances psychic abilities and offers protection during moonlit rituals.

WHITE Symbolizing purity and new beginnings, white is ideal for cleansing rituals and meditation, inviting peace and clarity.

BLUE Blue echoes the moon's calming qualities, promoting relaxation, emotional healing, and truth in your practices.

Other colors can also support lunar work, each bringing unique attributes:

RED Red represents passion, courage, and strength. Use it to boost energy and motivation, especially during the full moon to take decisive action.

ORANGE Orange symbolizes creativity, enthusiasm, and joy. Incorporate it during the waxing moon phase to stimulate growth or support career-related goals.

YELLOW Associated with intellect, happiness, and clarity, use yellow to brighten your mind, inspire new ideas, or clarify your intentions.

GREEN Green represents growth and healing, ideal for grounding and prosperity during any phase, but especially the waxing moon.

PURPLE Associated with spirituality, transformation, and psychic abilities, use purple during the waning moon to facilitate spiritual growth and intuitive insights.

PINK Representing love, compassion, and nurturing, incorporate pink to foster self-love, emotional healing, and harmonious relationships.

BLACK Associated with protection, banishing, and grounding, use black during the new moon to remove negative times of change.

GRAY Representing neutrality and balance, gray is ideal for resolving conflicts and finding equilibrium, particularly during the third quarter moon.

CRYSTALS

Crystals are valued for their ability to store, amplify, and transmit energy, making them powerful tools in rituals and personal practices. When used with intention, they can strengthen the connection between the physical and metaphysical worlds. By choosing stones that align with your goals, you can direct energy more effectively and enhance the impact of your spiritual work.

The following crystals are closely tied to lunar energy, but feel free to explore others that resonate with you. For example, during the action-driven first quarter phase, a motivation-boosting stone like carnelian might be just what you need.

MOONSTONE

Known for its connection to the moon and feminine energy, moonstone supports new beginnings and emotional balance, perfect for new moon rituals to set intentions and start fresh.

SELENITE

Selenite channels high-frequency energy to clarify the mind and elevate the spirit, making it ideal for full moon meditations to connect with lunar energies and enhance psychic awareness.

LABRADORITE

Labradorite shields against negativity and awakens intuitive abilities, it is useful during the waning moon to help release unwanted energies and foster transformative healing.

PEARL

Embodying purity and nurturing qualities, pearl can stabilize emotions during crescent moon phases, promoting serenity and emotional alignment. Its connection to feminine energy also supports gentle and nourishing self-care practices.

OPAL

Opal amplifies emotional states and enhances consciousness, which makes it suitable for waxing moon phases to nurture growth and boost creativity in personal projects.

CLEAR QUARTZ

A master healer, clear quartz amplifies energies and intentions, serving as a powerful tool for full moon ceremonies to magnify manifesting and healing work.

AQUAMARINE

Known for its calming properties, aquamarine eases stress, and is perfect for quarter moon rituals. It helps clarify the path ahead and soothes emotional turbulence, instilling hope, courage, and trust in the universe.

AMETHYST

Amethyst's soothing properties encourage relaxation, deep sleep, and peaceful dreams. Keep it under your pillow during the full moon to promote dream recall and connect to your intuitive wisdom.

SMOKY QUARTZ

Grounding and detoxifying, smoky quartz is excellent for waning moon phases, helping to release old patterns and ground spiritual energy into the physical realm.

LAPIS LAZULI

Enhancing truth and self-awareness, lapis lazuli can be used during the waxing gibbous moon to encourage honesty and clarity in advancing personal goals.

OBSIDIAN

A powerful protector and truth-enhancer, obsidian is ideal for shadow work during the waning moon phases, helping to uncover hidden truths and heal past traumas.

FLOWERS AND HERBS

Herbs and flowers hold unique energies that can beautifully align with moon magic, making them potent tools for tapping into lunar influences. Each plant carries specific correspondences that resonate with different phases of the moon, enhancing rituals and spells by drawing on these natural energies. By integrating these botanicals into your lunar practices, you can deepen your connection to the moon's cycles and amplify your intentions.

MOONFLOWER	Known for enhancing psychic abilities and promoting peaceful sleep, moonflower can be used during full moon rituals to deepen meditative states and connect with higher consciousness.
LEMON BALM	A calming herb that reduces stress and lifts spirits, lemon balm is perfect for new moon rituals aimed at setting intentions for emotional balance and spiritual renewal.
JASMINE	With its sweet aroma, jasmine boosts self-esteem and promotes love and prosperity. It can be incorporated into waxing moon rituals to attract positive relationships and stimulate financial growth.

LAVENDER	Lavender aids relaxation and purification, making it ideal for waning moon ceremonies to release tension and cleanse negative energies from your aura.
MILK THISTLE	Known for its protective qualities, milk thistle can be used during the waning moon to shield against psychic attack and facilitate spiritual detoxification.
ANISE	This star-shaped herb enhances clairvoyance and wards off evil. Use anise during the full moon to strengthen your protective barriers and amplify divination practices.
CLARY SAGE	Clary sage opens the third eye and aligns the spiritual body, making it useful in quarter moon rituals to enhance insight and support astral projection.
BLUE LOTUS	A sacred flower for spiritual rebirth, blue lotus is effective during the new moon for deepening meditation and renewing inner peace.
HIBISCUS	Hibiscus activates passion and self-love, making it suitable for first quarter moon rituals to initiate action on personal desires and creative projects.
WHITE POPPY	Known for inducing peaceful and prophetic dreams, white poppy can be utilized during the waning moon to facilitate restorative sleep and gain insights into emotional healing.

OILS AND INCENSE

These oils and incenses can be used individually or blended to enhance their effects. Incorporating them into your moon magic practices helps create a conducive atmosphere for ritual work that supports your intentions.

Here are a couple of ways to integrate these elements into your practices:

Start by anointing yourself or candles with oils tailored to your intentions. For example, use rose oil for love during a new moon, or sandalwood for protection. Similarly, burning specific incenses, like frankincense to raise spiritual vibrations or cinnamon to attract prosperity, can enhance the ritual's atmosphere and align your practice with the moon's energies.

FRANKINCENSE	Frankincense elevates consciousness and enhances meditation, perfect for full moon rituals to deepen your connection to the spiritual realm.
BLUE LOTUS	Known for its sedative and euphoric properties, blue lotus serves well in new moon rituals to promote spiritual opening and deepen meditative insights.

JASMINE	Jasmine attracts spiritual love and prosperity, suitable for waxing moon phases to draw in abundance and enhance romantic desires.
ROSE	Rose opens the heart chakra and nurtures emotional healing, excellent during the full moon to harmonize relationships and encourage self-love.
MYRRH	Myrrh purifies the environment and lifts vibrations, great for waning moon rituals to clear out negative energies and promote healing.
VERVAIN	Vervain stimulates creativity and protection, best used during the first quarter moon to initiate protective spells and inspire new projects.
SANDALWOOD	Sandalwood promotes calmness and spiritual insight, ideal for quarter moon meditations to maintain balance and harmony.
POPPY	Poppy induces relaxation and enhances dreams, perfect for the dark moon or new moon to facilitate restful sleep and receive prophetic dreams.
ROSEMARY	Rosemary enhances mental clarity and purification, suitable for the waxing crescent moon to set clear intentions and cleanse the aura of past baggage.
YLANG-YLANG	Ylang-Ylang boosts joy and sensual energy, effective during the full moon to celebrate achievements and heighten emotional and sensual pleasures.

LUNAR DEITIES

Lunar deities from various cultures embody qualities that can enhance your moon magic. This list highlights a few popular examples, but many cultures have their own lunar deities with unique attributes, so feel free to explore and connect with those that resonate most with you and your personal practice.

HECATE | Greek

The goddess of magic, witchcraft, the night, and ghosts, Hecate is often associated with the waning moon. She protects all who stand at the crossroads and is powerful for magic involving wisdom, protection, and guidance through transitions.

DIANA | Roman

Associated with wild animals and woodlands, Diana is a lunar goddess and a protector of the wild. She symbolizes the connection between moon magic and nature; her energy is potent for protection and fertility spells. Her equivalent in Greek mythology is Artemis.

ARTEMIS | Greek

Artemis is the goddess of the hunt, wilderness, and childbirth. She is often depicted with a crescent moon crown, symbolizing her role as a protector and her connection to wildlife and the moon. She is ideal for rituals of strength, independence, and protection during new beginnings.

LUNA | Roman

In Roman mythology, Luna is the moon's divine embodiment. She represents the moon's phases and controls its movements. She is often depicted as the female counterpart to the sun god, Sol. During the full moon, her energy is ideal for rituals promoting balance, emotional well-being, and heightened intuition.

SELENE | Greek

The goddess of the moon, Selene, is seen as a personification of the moon itself and is often depicted driving a chariot across the night sky. Invoking Selene in rituals can enhance clarity, fertility, and intuition.

CERIDWEN | Celtic

Ceridwen, the goddess of transformation and wisdom, is linked to the moon through her cauldron, which symbolizes rebirth. She is suitable for knowledge and self-transformation spells.

ISIS | Egyptian

A central goddess in Egyptian mythology, Isis is associated with healing, protection, and magic. Invoke her during crescent moon rituals to harness her healing prowess.

CHAPTER

4

LUNAR RITUALS AND SPELLS

Now that you've familiarized yourself with the vast array of tools available for lunar work, it's time to dive deeper and apply what you've learned. In this chapter, we'll build on that foundation with tips, tools, and empowering rituals designed to harness the unique energies of each lunar phase.

This chapter is organized into eight sections, each aligned with a different phase of the moon. Within each section, you'll find rituals specific to that phase's energy, complete with guidance on areas to focus on, common challenges to be aware of, and affirmations to help maintain your focus. Additionally, I suggest crystals, herbs, and other items that can amplify your practices.

Building on the structured rituals, the general meditations and visualizations outlined in each section can stand alone for those times when your schedule is tight, or they can serve as an energetic primer for any moon phase ritual, enhancing your connection to the moon's energy. If you find an affirmation that resonates, feel free to weave it into your rituals or repeat it daily throughout the phase.

BEFORE YOU BEGIN

Before you dive into the lunar spells and rituals, it's important to know that there is no single "right" way to approach your practice—what matters most is that it feels meaningful to you. To help you get the most out of these rituals, here are a few practical tips to keep in mind as you begin your lunar journey:

START SMALL

Don't feel pressured to use every tool or perform every ritual. Think of this book as a resource, not a checklist to complete. If you're new to this practice or short on time, begin by reading the recommended focus points for each phase to familiarize yourself with the energies at play. From there, try a meditation or visualization exercise—simple, mini rituals that require no materials.

PERSONALIZE YOUR PRACTICE

Tailor rituals and tools to fit your individual needs. Adjust affirmations to reflect your intentions, and swap out tools for those that resonate with you. If you don't have a particular crystal or herb that is listed, you can use clear quartz and rosemary as general substitutes for any crystal and herb.

FOLLOW YOUR INTUITION

Let your intuition guide your practice. These rituals are meant to feel inspired, not forced. Don't stress about achieving perfection or adhering to strict schedules—trust your instincts. If a ritual doesn't resonate with you, skip or modify it to align with your energy.

Remember, this journey is yours to shape. Approach it with curiosity and openness, and allow your rituals to evolve alongside you.

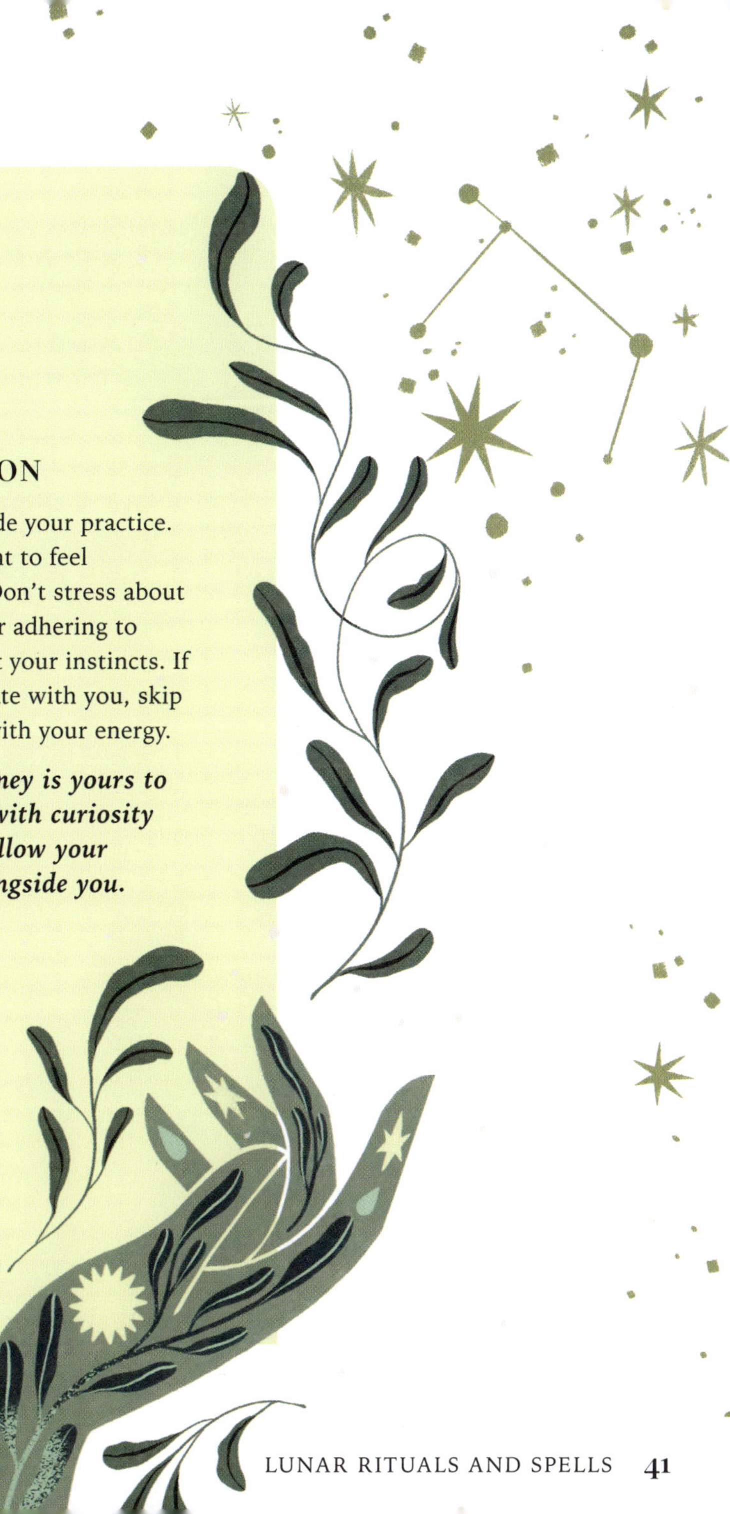

PHASE 1

THE NEW MOON

BEGINNINGS AND INTENTIONS

BEST FOR

Setting intentions, visualization, planting seeds for new projects

The new moon is all about fresh starts and setting intentions. This phase marks the beginning of the lunar cycle, offering you a blank slate to plant the seeds of your desires. It's a time to get clear on what you want to manifest in the coming weeks. Whether starting a new project, setting personal goals, or simply taking a moment to realign your focus, the new moon encourages you to dream big and embrace the possibilities. Use this energy to lay the groundwork for growth, keeping your intentions positive and forward-focused.

PREPARING FOR
THE NEW MOON

As the new moon ushers in a fresh start, it creates a powerful opportunity for setting intentions and clearing out what no longer serves you. This phase is about embracing the stillness and darkness, using them as a fertile ground to plant the seeds of your deepest desires. To align with the new moon's energy, consider incorporating these grounding and introspective tools into your practices to enhance your focus and intention-setting.

WHAT TO FOCUS ON
DURING THE NEW MOON

Setting Clear Intentions

The new moon provides a blank slate, making it the perfect time to define your goals and desires. Focus on what you truly want to manifest in your life. Ambiguity can dilute your intentions, so be specific and deliberate in your thought process.

Embracing Change and Flexibility

The new moon is synonymous with new beginnings. Be open to unexpected opportunities that may arise. Flexibility allows you to adapt and make the most of the new energy, turning potential challenges into stepping stones.

Protecting Your Energy

You may be more sensitive to the energies around you during this time. Protect your space by limiting interactions with people who drain you. This may mean saying no to social invitations or taking a social media break. It's okay to set boundaries.

WHAT TO AVOID
DURING THE NEW MOON

Skipping Self-Care

The new moon's energy can be intense, making it important to maintain your physical and emotional well-being. Avoid neglecting self-care; instead, engage in activities that replenish your energy and keep you balanced.

Doubting the Process

It's easy to become impatient when you don't see immediate results from your new moon intentions. Avoid doubting the process. Trust that each step contributes to your desired outcomes, even if progress isn't immediately visible.

Overloading Your Schedule

The new moon is not the time to overwhelm yourself with too many tasks or commitments. Instead, focus on a few key intentions or projects that are truly important to you. This will help you direct your energy more effectively and prevent burnout.

CRYSTALS

Moonstone

For enhancing intuition and connecting with the energy of new beginnings.

Labradorite

For protection and setting the stage for transformation.

Black Tourmaline

For grounding and clearing away negative energy.

HERBS AND INCENSE

Sage

For cleansing your space and mind, creating a blank slate for new intentions.

Lavender

For calming the mind and aiding in clarity and peaceful intention-setting.

Rosemary

For purification and mental clarity as you focus on your new goals.

ITEMS

New Moon Symbols

Add items to your space that represent new beginnings, such as a blank canvas or an empty bowl.

Cleansing Tools

Keep cleansing items like salt, crystals, or sacred water nearby to clear away lingering energies.

Journals and Pens

Use a fresh journal to write down your intentions, dreams, and plans for the upcoming cycle.

NEW MOON

MEDITATION AND VISUALIZATION

New Moon Meditation for Cleansing

Find a quiet place where you can sit comfortably. Close your eyes and begin to breathe deeply, inhaling through your nose and exhaling through your mouth. As you breathe, imagine the dark sky of the new moon overhead, symbolizing a clean slate.

With each exhale, release any negative energy and stress. Envision these elements dissolving into the ground beneath you. With each inhale, invite in fresh, pure energy, feeling it cleanse your mind, body, and spirit. Continue this cycle of cleansing breaths for a few minutes. Finish by silently affirming your readiness for new beginnings.

New Moon Visualization for Renewal

Find a quiet space where you can relax and close your eyes. Begin with deep, calming breaths to center yourself. Picture yourself under the dark canvas of the new moon, surrounded by an open, starlit sky. Imagine holding a seed in your hands—this represents your new intentions or beginnings.

As you breathe in deeply, visualize planting this seed in the fertile ground. With each exhale, imagine the seed slowly growing, nourished by your focused energy and the nurturing darkness of the new moon. Feel a connection to the potential of your intentions as they begin to take root. When you're ready, slowly open your eyes, carrying the sense of new beginnings with you, and trusting that your intentions are planted and will grow in their own perfect time.

NEW MOON

AFFIRMATIONS

I am fully aligned with my highest potential.

My intentions are clear and I am committed to realizing them.

I am worthy of the dreams I aspire to achieve.

Every step I take is supported by the universe.

I embrace new beginnings with an open mind and heart.

Abundance surrounds me.

NEW MOON

RITUALS

And so it begins. We start our journey in the lunar cycle with the new moon. There's something undeniably magical about the darkness and stillness of this phase. So, I ask you: what is quietly stirring within you? What dreams or inspirations are beginning to take shape, waiting for the right moment to grow? This phase invites you to step into the unknown with trust, knowing that the universe is listening. It's not about limits; it's about allowing yourself to imagine without boundaries.

The new moon is your invitation to start fresh, to clear away anything that feels stagnant or heavy, and to create the space your dreams need to flourish. These rituals will guide you in aligning with this energy—helping you make room for the new, nurturing your intentions, and setting powerful groundwork for the weeks ahead. As you work through these practices, give yourself permission to dream freely, knowing that this is your time to plant seeds that will blossom in the days to come.

CREATING A NEW BEGINNINGS ALTAR

MATERIALS

- A small table or surface for your altar
- Fresh flowers or budding plants
- Manifestation crystals (such as green aventurine, citrine)
- Symbols of growth (such as seeds, leaves, new moon imagery)
- Incense or essential oils

1. Start by choosing a quiet and personal space for your altar, a place where you can focus on your intentions for new beginnings. Lay a green or white cloth on the surface if desired, symbolizing growth and purity.
2. Arrange fresh flowers or a budding plant on the altar to represent the new opportunities and growth you are inviting into your life. Place crystals associated with manifestation and success, like green aventurine or citrine, around the flowers. Include symbols of growth, such as seeds or leaves, and an image or representation of the new moon to honor the lunar phase. Light incense or diffuse essential oils to create a serene and focused atmosphere.
3. As you arrange each item, focus on your goals and intentions, visualizing them growing and flourishing. Spend a few moments each day at your altar, reflecting on your intentions and allowing the positive energy to inspire and guide you. This ritual helps to anchor your goals in a physical space, making your intentions tangible and ever-present in your daily life.

MATERIALS

- Incense
- Matches or a lighter
- A white candle
- Crystals you wish to charge
- A piece of soft cloth
- Singing bowl or chime

CRYSTAL CHARGING CEREMONY

1. Begin by cleansing your space with your incense of choice, creating a pure and sacred environment. Light the white candle to symbolize light and clarity, setting a peaceful atmosphere.
2. Lay your crystals out on a soft cloth, arranging them so they do not touch each other, ensuring each crystal is fully charged.
3. If you have a singing bowl, gently strike it and let the sound waves flow over your crystals, imbuing them with vibrations that enhance their natural properties. Alternatively, use a chime to cast sound vibrations.
4. As the sound fills the air, visualize each crystal glowing with renewed energy, ready to assist you in your intentions for the lunar cycle. Hold each crystal in your hand briefly and set a specific intention for it, whether for healing, protection, or inspiration.
5. Let the crystals sit near the candle for at least ten minutes before carefully snuffing out the candle. You can also let the candle burn down completely, as long as you supervise it. This simple ceremony ensures your crystals are not only recharged but also primed to operate at peak performance, supporting your intentions throughout the entire lunar cycle.

SMOKE CLEANSING WAND RITUAL FOR PURIFICATION

MATERIALS

- 4 sprigs of dried garden sage
- 4 sprigs of dried rosemary
- 4 sprigs of dried lavender
- Natural ribbon or twine
- Matches or a lighter
- A fireproof container or shell

1. Start by gathering four sprigs of each herb: garden sage (to dispel negativity), rosemary (for protection), and lavender (for tranquility). Bind these herbs tightly together with natural ribbon or twine. As you tie the wand, focus on clearing your space and aura of any negative or stagnant energies. You can also repeat an affirmation at this time that supports your intention for purification.
2. Ignite the tip of the wand with matches or a lighter, allowing it to smolder. Gently blow out any flames to produce smoke. Ensure your windows are open to aid ventilation and the dispersal of negative energy. Using a fireproof container to hold the smoldering wand, start at your home's front door and move clockwise through each room. Wave the smoke into all corners and around windows to thoroughly purify the space. Visualize the smoke absorbing negativity and bringing peace and protection.
3. Circle the smoke wand around your body from head to toe, cleansing your personal energy field. Once completed, extinguish the wand by pressing it into the fireproof container.
4. Dispose of the used herbs respectfully, preferably by returning them to nature. This ritual refreshes your living space and aura, to create an environment where positive energies thrive.

PHASE 2

THE WAXING CRESCENT MOON

SETTING FOUNDATIONS

BEST FOR

Planning and strategy, creating actionable to-do lists, researching and gathering resources

As the moon begins to grow in the sky, the waxing crescent phase brings a sense of momentum and possibility. This is the time to start taking small, actionable steps toward the goals you set during the new moon. Think of it as the "watering the seeds" phase, where your intentions begin to take root. The energy here is all about building, nurturing, and setting the stage for success. It's a great time to develop plans, gather resources, and stay committed to your vision. Even small progress can lead to significant results, so keep moving forward.

PREPARING FOR
THE WAXING CRESCENT MOON

While the new moon offered a quiet space for setting intentions and planting seeds of possibility, the waxing crescent invites you to take those first small, brave steps towards making your dreams a reality. This phase is all about initiation and gathering the energy needed to move forwards, so incorporating some of these energy-boosting and inspiring tools into your practices can help support and strengthen your intentions.

WHAT TO FOCUS ON

DURING THE WAXING CRESCENT MOON

Evaluate and Adjust

Start by reviewing the intentions you set during the new moon. Reflect on what you wrote, visualized, or meditated upon. As you gain clarity, you might feel the need to tweak or adjust your intentions. Make any necessary changes to ensure your intentions are clear, specific, and actionable.

Break Down Your Intentions

To make your intentions more manageable, break them down into smaller, actionable steps. These short-term goals should be achievable within the waxing crescent phase, giving you a clear roadmap for the next few days or weeks.

Learn and Expand

This is an excellent time to learn new skills or gather knowledge that supports your goals. Whether it's taking a course, reading a book, or seeking advice, expanding your knowledge base can provide you with valuable tools and insights for your journey.

WHAT TO AVOID

DURING THE WAXING CRESCENT MOON

Getting Stuck in Planning

While it's good to set intentions and make plans, spending too much time planning can hinder your ability to take action. Don't get bogged down in overanalyzing every detail. Instead, start taking small steps towards your goals.

Consuming Negative Media

Be mindful of the media you consume. Avoid news or entertainment that leaves you feeling anxious or pessimistic. Opt for uplifting and motivating content that reinforces your intentions.

Ignoring Small Opportunities

Avoid overlooking small opportunities because they seem insignificant. Keep an open mind and follow your curiosity, as you never know where it might take you.

CRYSTALS

Carnelian

For motivation and confidence in pursuing new goals.

Green Aventurine

For growth and prosperity.

Tiger's Eye

For courage and overcoming fears of the unknown.

HERBS AND INCENSE

Mugwort

For success and quick action.

Cinnamon

For motivation and energy.

Pine

For strength and steadiness.

ITEMS

Symbols of New Beginnings

Add items to your space that represent new beginnings, such as fresh flowers, young plants, or seeds.

Inspirational Elements

Surround yourself with objects that inspire and spark creativity, like vision boards, motivational quotes, or images that resonate with your goals.

Lights and Colors

Opt for bright and energizing lighting, such as candles or string lights. Wear colors like green, gold, or orange for renewal, abundance, and motivation.

MEDITATION AND VISUALIZATION

Waxing Crescent Moon Meditation for Expansion

Find a quiet place where you can sit comfortably. Close your eyes and take a few deep, calming breaths, inhaling through your nose and exhaling through your mouth. As you breathe, imagine your lungs expanding. Allow this sensation of expansion to ripple through your body, fostering openness and spaciousness within.

As thoughts arise, gently let them pass, focusing only on the sensation of your breath filling you with potential. On each inhale, silently think the word "expand". On each exhale, release any tension or resistance, mentally repeating "release". After a few minutes, set a clear intention for the growth you wish to nurture during this lunar phase, feeling empowered by your internal expansion.

Waxing Crescent Moon Visualization for Success

Find a peaceful spot where you can sit comfortably without distractions. Close your eyes and take slow, deep breaths. Inhale through your nose, pause briefly, then exhale gently through your mouth, letting go of tension with each breath.

Imagine yourself successfully achieving your goals. Visualize the details—the setting, the actions, and the people around you. Feel the emotions of joy, pride, and accomplishment as vividly as possible. Repeat affirmations like, "I am successful" and "I achieve my goals with ease", to reinforce your vision. When you are ready, gently return to the present, open your eyes, and carry this confidence forward.

WAXING CRESCENT MOON

AFFIRMATIONS

I nurture my intentions
with action and dedication.

My efforts are powerful
and productive.

Every small step contributes
to substantial growth.

I am motivated and
undeterred by challenges.

My journey is blessed
with continual progress.

Every obstacle I face is
an opportunity to
become stronger.

WAXING CRESCENT MOON

RITUALS

The new moon gave you a fresh start—a blank canvas where your dreams and intentions began to take shape. Now, with the waxing crescent, it's time to nurture those seeds and help them take root. This phase invites you to begin taking small, intentional actions that will bring your goals closer to reality. What steps can you take today, even if they seem small, to support your journey forward?

During the waxing crescent, momentum builds slowly but steadily. The energy is ripe for laying a strong foundation, committing to your intentions, and taking deliberate actions to bring them to life. The rituals in this section are designed to help you harness that forward motion, giving you the confidence and clarity to stay on course.

CREATING AN INSPIRED VISION BOARD

MATERIALS

- Scissors, glue, and markers
- Magazines, photos, and other visual materials
- A poster board or large piece of paper
- Markers, paint, stickers, and other decorative items (optional)

1. Start by gathering your materials in a clean space, then spend some quiet time reflecting on your dreams and objectives for the future. Consider all areas of your life, such as career, personal growth, relationships, health, and travel, and think about what you want to achieve.

2. Once you feel connected to your goals, start cutting out images and phrases from your collected materials that align with your aspirations. Look for images, words, and phrases that inspire you. Arrange these elements on your board, experimenting with different layouts until you find one that feels right. Don't rush this process; be creative and intuitive, letting it flow naturally.

3. After you're satisfied with the layout, glue everything in place. As you attach each item, focus on your intention for it, imagining how you will feel when these dreams and goals materialize. Once all the pieces are secured, you can add final touches with markers or paint.

4. Display your vision board in a place where you will see it regularly, such as your bedroom or workspace. This will help keep your goals at the forefront of your mind and inspire you to take actions that align with your visions. Look at your vision board everyday, visualizing achieving your goals.

MATERIALS

- A green or white candle
- Carving tool (small knife or pin)
- Essential oils (optional)
- A nonflammable surface
- Matches or a lighter

CANDLE CARVING RITUAL FOR EMPOWERING INTENTIONS

1. Begin by finding a quiet space where you can focus on your intentions without distractions. Hold your green or white candle, which symbolizes growth and new beginnings, and concentrate on your goals for this lunar cycle.
2. Using the carving tool, carefully inscribe words, symbols, or simple images on the candle that represent your intentions. These carvings can include keywords like "growth", "abundance", or "clarity", or symbols like stars, leaves, hearts, or other personal sigils. If desired, anoint the candle with a few drops of essential oil, rubbing it from wick to base to seal in your intentions. Choose energizing oils, such as citrus scents like lemon or bergamot, or invigorating ones like eucalyptus or peppermint.
3. Place the candle on a safe, heat-resistant surface and light it, visualizing your goals manifesting as the flame grows brighter. As the candle burns, focus on the energy being released, empowering your carved intentions and igniting motivation. Allow the candle to burn out naturally, if safe to do so (never leave a lit candle unattended), or snuff it out and relight it daily until fully burned.

MATERIALS

- Small piece of paper and a pen (optional)
- Small pots or a garden plot
- Potting soil
- Seeds of your choice (flowers, herbs, or vegetables)
- Watering can or spray bottle

Tip: *If you're not confident in your gardening skills or are worried about keeping plants alive, consider starting with low-maintenance options like succulents or cacti that are fully grown and ready to use. These plants still offer a meaningful way to engage with this ritual.*

SEEDS OF CHANGE RITUAL FOR NURTURING GROWTH

1. Begin by choosing a quiet and mindful time for your planting, allowing yourself to connect deeply with your intentions. If desired, write down specific goals or intentions on a small piece of paper, folding it, and setting it aside.
2. Fill your pots with potting soil, or prepare your garden plot by loosening the soil. As you hold the seeds in your hands, take a moment to focus on what you wish to manifest in your life, infusing each seed with your intentions. If you wrote your intentions on paper, place it at the bottom of the pot or bury it lightly in the soil, covering it with a bit more soil.
3. Plant the seeds according to the instructions for depth and spacing, gently covering them with soil. As you water the seeds, visualize your intentions growing and coming to fruition, nurtured by your care and the natural elements. Place the pots in a sunny spot or ensure your garden plot receives adequate sunlight.
4. Continue to water and care for your plants regularly, using their growth as a reminder of your intentions and the energy you are cultivating in your life.

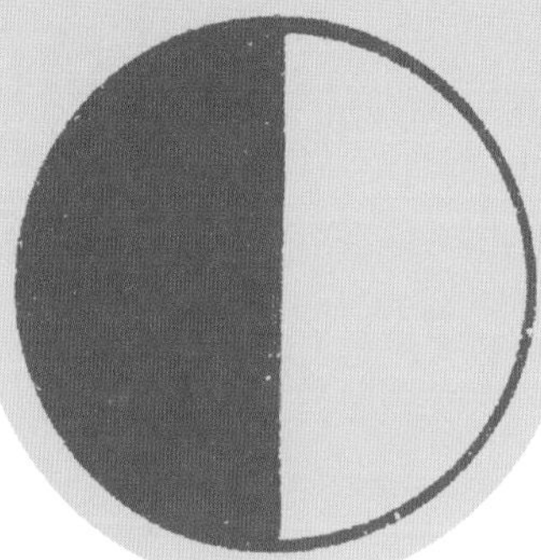

PHASE 3

THE FIRST QUARTER MOON

DECISION AND ACTION

BEST FOR

Problem-solving, building momentum, tackling challenges head-on

The first quarter moon acts as a checkpoint in the lunar cycle, where you can assess how things are going with your goals. The energy of this phase is dynamic and action-oriented, pushing you to make decisions and overcome any obstacles that may have popped up. It's a time to refine your approach, address challenges head-on, and solidify your commitment. This phase is about resilience and determination—if you've hit a snag, now's the time to push through. Use the first quarter energy to stay focused and keep your momentum strong.

PREPARING FOR
THE FIRST QUARTER MOON

As the first quarter moon ascends, it's essential to prepare both your mental and physical spaces to harness its dynamic energy. This phase signals a time of action and overcoming obstacles, making it crucial to fortify your environment with empowering and symbolic elements that resonate with the moon's assertive energies.

WHAT TO FOCUS ON

DURING THE FIRST QUARTER MOON

Assess Resources

Evaluate what you have and what you need to accomplish your goals. This might involve securing additional materials, seeking expertise, or rearranging your schedule to prioritize essential activities. Ensuring you have the right resources in place can boost your efficiency and effectiveness.

Strengthen Commitment

Reinforce your dedication to your goals. Remind yourself why you started and what you hope to achieve. This commitment can be your anchor during challenging times, helping you remain focused and driven.

Stay Positive

It's normal to encounter resistance during this phase. Instead of getting frustrated by obstacles, view them as opportunities to learn and grow. Overcoming each obstacle brings you closer to your goals.

WHAT TO AVOID

DURING THE FIRST QUARTER MOON

Hesitating on Choices

This phase is about taking decisive action. Avoid wavering on decisions or second-guessing yourself. Trust your judgment and commit to your choices to maintain forward momentum—don't get stuck in analysis paralysis.

Inflexibility

While determination is important, being overly rigid can prevent you from adapting to new information or changing circumstances. Avoid stubbornness and be willing to adjust your plans as needed.

Ignoring Feedback

Constructive feedback is valuable during this phase. Avoid dismissing advice or insights from others. Be open to different perspectives that can help you overcome obstacles more effectively.

CRYSTALS

Red Jasper

For stamina and perseverance.

Bloodstone

For vitality and courage.

Sunstone

For leadership and strength.

HERBS AND INCENSE

Ginger

For energizing and encouraging progress.

Peppermint

For determination and focus.

Rosemary

For mental clarity and protection.

ITEMS

Symbols of Strength

Integrate items that represent strength and fortitude, such as robust plants or images of mountains.

Motivational Elements

Fill your space with items that ignite your determination and drive. This could include symbols of past achievements, motivational quotes, or objects that represent your goals, like a small trophy or an item tied to your ambitions.

Bright and Stimulating Lights

Employ vibrant lighting, like bright candles or colorful lights, to energize your space. Choose colors like red, orange, and yellow to invoke the energizing influence of the first quarter moon.

MEDITATION AND VISUALIZATION

First Quarter Moon Meditation for Strength

Choose a quiet space where you can sit comfortably. Close your eyes and start by taking deep, grounding breaths to center yourself in the present moment.

As you continue to breathe deeply, recall a moment in your life when you felt particularly strong and empowered. Hold this memory in your mind, focusing on the feelings of strength and confidence it evokes. With each inhale, draw these feelings into your core, filling yourself with resilience and power. With each exhale, release any self-doubt or uncertainty, letting these feelings leave your body and mind.

Maintain this focus and allow the empowered feeling to grow with each breath cycle, reinforcing your internal fortitude. As you conclude your meditation, carry this sense of strength and readiness forward throughout your day.

First Quarter Moon Visualization for Overcoming Obstacles

In a tranquil environment, relax and close your eyes, beginning with deep, grounding breaths. Visualize yourself on a path facing a series of gates or barriers. In your hands, imagine holding a key—this represents the solutions and strategies you possess.

As you breathe in deeply, see yourself approaching the first gate. With each exhale, use your key to unlock the barrier, effectively overcoming your challenges. Feel a sense of accomplishment grow with each step forward, as your path clears and your goals become more attainable.

FIRST QUARTER MOON

AFFIRMATIONS

I trust myself to make clear and confident decisions.

I am adaptable and resourceful, finding solutions to every challenge that arises.

I have everything I need to succeed.

I use obstacles to motivate me to learn and grow.

I am strong, independent, and thriving.

I free myself from all self-destructive doubts, fears, and limiting beliefs.

FIRST QUARTER MOON

RITUALS

As you transition from the nurturing energy of the waxing crescent into the dynamic first quarter moon, the seeds you've planted are starting to sprout. But for them to truly thrive, their roots must run deep. This is the phase where you check in with your progress and ensure that your foundation is solid. How are things going with the goals you've set? Are your plans running smoothly, or have you hit a snag? The rituals in this section are designed to help you adjust your strategy, strengthen your resilience, and tackle challenges head-on so you can keep moving forward.

COURAGE-IN-A-CUP POTION FOR CONQUERING FEARS

MATERIALS

- Candle or incense (optional)
- 2 cups (500ml) filtered water
- A small pot
- 1in (2½cm) ginger root (peeled and sliced)
- 1 tbsp peppermint leaves (fresh or dried)
- Strainer
- Mug or ceremonial cup
- 1 tbsp honey for sweetness (optional)

1. Begin by lighting a candle or incense to create a focused and sacred atmosphere. Pour the filtered water into your pot and bring it to a simmer.
2. Hold the ginger root slices and peppermint leaves in your hands; to infuse them with your intention for courage and decisive action.
3. Add the ginger and peppermint to the pot then gently simmer for about ten minutes, stirring occasionally. Visualize the steam carrying away your self-doubt, leaving behind a brew enriched with bravery, strength, and confidence.
4. Remove the pot from the heat and allow to steep for a few minutes. Strain the potion into your mug, adding honey if desired to sweeten the potion.
5. Cradle the cup with both hands. Before drinking, reaffirm your intention, charging the potion with your desire for courage. As you sip slowly, visualize your obstacle shrinking, growing smaller with every sip until it disappears completely.
6. Once you've finished the potion, take a moment to focus on the renewed sense of vitality and purpose filling your spirit. Consider tackling the most daunting item on your to-do list first. The power of the potion, now coursing through you, will bolster your resolve, allowing you to confront your challenges without fear.

MATERIALS

- A yellow candle
- Matches or a lighter
- A piece of citrine
- A comfortable mat or cushion

SOLAR PLEXUS CHAKRA ACTIVATION RITUAL FOR PERSONAL POWER

1. Find a quiet space where you can sit comfortably without disturbances.
2. Light the yellow candle to represent the element of fire, associated with the solar plexus chakra, and set the intention of igniting your inner power.
3. Place the piece of citrine, or another yellow crystal of your choice, in front of you or hold it in your hands.
4. Sit on the mat or cushion and take a few deep breaths to center yourself. Focus on the area just above your navel, where the solar plexus chakra resides. Visualize a bright yellow light at this spot, growing brighter and more vibrant with each breath. Feel the warmth from the light spreading throughout your body, empowering and energizing you.
5. Hold the crystal while continuing to visualize the yellow light. Imagine it spinning clockwise, gaining momentum, and clearing any blockages. You might find it helpful to silently or audibly affirm, "I am powerful, confident, and in control of my life."
6. Continue this meditation for about 5–10 minutes, or as long as feels comfortable. Afterward, carefully snuff out the candle, carrying forward the energy and confidence you've cultivated.

MATERIALS

- A candle or incense (optional)
- Your preferred tarot deck
- Notebook and pen

TAROT SPREAD FOR DECISION-MAKING

1. Find an area to sit undisturbed. Light a candle or some incense to enhance focus and invite spiritual guidance.
2. Shuffle your tarot deck slowly, channeling your intention to uncover clear insights into your paths.
3. When ready, lay out the cards as below:
   Card 1 (Center): The core issue or nature of the decision.
   Card 2 (Left of center): Potential outcomes of the first path or option.
   Card 3 (Right of center): Potential outcomes of the second path or option.
   Card 4 (Above center): External factors affecting the decision.
   Card 5 (Below center): Subconscious or hidden aspects influencing your choice.
4. As you review each card, consider both the direct meanings and how the symbols and imagery relate to your situation. Is there a recurring theme or figure appearing in the spread? What gut reactions do you have toward them? Use your notebook to jot down any insights.
5. Before concluding, spend a moment to reflect on the spread as a whole. What story do the cards tell when viewed together? Finally, trust your intuition; tarot taps into your inner wisdom, and often, your first impression holds the key to your true feelings about the paths ahead.

PHASE 4

THE WAXING GIBBOUS MOON

REFINEMENT AND PERSEVERANCE

BEST FOR

Organizing, fine-tuning, preparing for completion, reviewing progress

As the moon grows fuller, the waxing gibbous phase invites you to fine-tune and perfect your plans. This is the phase of refinement, where you make adjustments and polish the work you've done so far. The energy here is one of anticipation and preparation—you're getting closer to the culmination of your efforts. It's a great time to review your progress, make any necessary tweaks, and ensure that everything is aligned with your intentions. This phase encourages patience and perseverance, helping you get everything in place before the full moon's peak.

PREPARING FOR
THE WAXING GIBBOUS MOON

As the waxing gibbous moon rises, it's vital to tune both your mind and environment to its powerful energy. This phase, drawing close to full illumination, focuses on refinement and final adjustments, making it essential to enhance your surroundings with elements that support insight and precision.

WHAT TO FOCUS ON

DURING THE WAXING GIBBOUS MOON

Reviewing Your Work

Use this phase to review progress, make necessary adjustments, and fine-tune details—whether you're reworking a business plan, revising an article, or perfecting a creative piece.

Pre-Launch Polish

If you're preparing for an important event or meeting, this is a great time for final practice runs or rehearsals. The increasing light of this phase also enhances public visibility. Begin to share teasers or previews of upcoming projects or launches to build excitement and anticipation.

Checking in with Allies

Connect with colleagues, mentors, or friends who are supportive of your goals. Discuss your progress, share your concerns, and gather feedback. This engagement can provide you with valuable insights and encouragement as you approach the culmination of your efforts.

WHAT TO AVOID

DURING THE WAXING GIBBOUS MOON

Falling into Perfection Paralysis

This phase of the moon can heighten attention to detail, but don't let perfectionism halt your progress. Use this time to advance, rather than obsess over imperfections that only you notice.

Resisting Necessary Adjustments

When feedback points to a need for change, avoid rigidity or stubbornness. This phase supports dynamic adjustments, allowing you to update and improve your strategies based on the latest inputs.

Starting New Projects

Keep your attention on finalizing and perfecting what's already in progress. New initiatives should wait, as they could lead to scattered efforts and undermine the success of work already in motion.

CRYSTALS

Chrysocolla

For clear communication and expressing ideas.

Fluorite

For organization and dissolving confusion.

Lapis Lazuli

For wisdom and truth.

HERBS AND INCENSE

Lemon Balm

For soothing stress and attracting success.

Oregano

For joy and letting go of tension.

Sandalwood

For mental clarity and calmness before manifestation.

ITEMS

Symbols of Completion

Incorporate items that symbolize fulfillment and accomplishment, such as completed lists or models of finished projects.

Reflective Elements

Use mirrors to reflect on past efforts and visualize the successful completion of your goals.

Enhancing Aromas

For grounding and clearing away negative energy to make space for fresh starts.

MEDITATION AND VISUALIZATION

Waxing Gibbous Moon Meditation for Commitment

Find a quiet space, sit comfortably, and close your eyes. Take a few deep breaths to center yourself. Visualize the nearly full moon shining brightly above you, symbolizing the nearing completion of your goals. With each inhale, draw in focus and determination; with each exhale, release doubt and hesitation. Silently repeat, "I am committed to my path. My dedication brings my goals to fruition." Feel a sense of calm certainty wash over you as the moon's energy strengthens your commitment to seeing things through.

Waxing Gibbous Moon Visualization for Achievement

Settle into a comfortable space, close your eyes, and take deep breaths to ground yourself. Imagine you're in the final stretch of a long-distance race. Visualize the path ahead, the beat of your powerful and purposeful footsteps syncing with your heartbeat. Feel the exhilaration as you near the finish line, the crowd's cheers growing louder. Picture yourself crossing that line in triumphant victory, arms raised, heart swelling with pride. Allow yourself to bask in this moment of glory, internalizing the success as you whisper, "I am unstoppable; I achieve my goals." Slowly open your eyes, carrying this winning energy into your reality as you make your final preparations.

WAXING GIBBOUS MOON

AFFIRMATIONS

Everything is falling perfectly into place for me.

I am committed to completing what I've started.

My patience and persistence bring me closer to my desired outcome.

I embrace the small adjustments that lead to significant results.

My attention to detail ensures quality and excellence in all I do.

I fine-tune my efforts with clarity and focus.

WAXING GIBBOUS MOON

RITUALS

As we approach the waxing gibbous moon, we find ourselves in a unique phase distinct from the earlier stages of the waxing cycle. While energy continues to grow, it now teeters on the brink of reaching its zenith. This phase marks a critical threshold where the expansive surge of the waxing phases meets the culmination point, setting the stage for the total illumination of the full moon. The following rituals can help to prepare you for the peak manifestations that are just on the horizon.

THE LUNAR SUCCESS SCRIPT FOR WRITING YOUR DREAMS INTO REALITY

MATERIALS

- Blue paper
- A silver pen
- A piece of moonstone

1. Begin by finding a tranquil space where you can sit undisturbed under the moonlight, outside or near a window. Meditate on your current goals and dreams. Think about what you'd like to manifest in vivid detail, focusing on what success looks like and feels like to you.
2. Write a description of your life as if all your goals have been achieved, using the present tense so the words feel current and real. Blue paper represents the moon's influence and a silver pen symbolizes lunar energy. As you write, visualize each success unfolding. Once completed, read your script aloud while holding the moonstone (which enhances lunar connection), allowing its energy to open up a realm of endless possibilities.
3. Fold the paper and keep it somewhere you can regularly revisit to reinforce your intentions.
4. Close your ritual by reflecting under the moonlight, feeling gratitude for the clarity and inspiration it provides. This reflection process helps solidify the connection between your intentions and their manifestation. To enhance the ritual's impact, return to your script during each full moon. Read it aloud to reaffirm your goals and add any new aspirations as your desires evolve.

GOAL-GETTER OIL BLEND FOR MOTIVATION

MATERIALS

- Carrier oil (such as almond or jojoba oil)
- A 1oz (30ml) mixing bottle or vial
- Peppermint, ginger, and cedarwood essential oils
- Label and pen

1. Begin by selecting a quiet and clean space. Start with your carrier oil as the base—this will dilute the essential oils and make them safe for skin application. Pour your carrier oil into the small mixing bottle until it is nearly filled.
2. Add five drops of peppermint oil to the bottle to invigorate the mind and enhance focus. Include three drops of ginger oil to stimulate inner warmth and increase energy levels, supporting persistent efforts. Finally, mix in four drops of cedarwood oil for its grounding properties, which help stabilize and sustain your long-term commitment.
3. Cap the bottle and shake gently to blend the oils thoroughly. Label your bottle with the name of the blend and the date. Before using, hold the bottle in your hands, close your eyes, and repeat the affirmation: "With every breath, I renew my commitment to my goals and strengthen my resolve." This helps charge the oil with your intentions.
4. Apply a small amount of the oil blend to your wrists or the back of your neck while reaffirming your intentions for perseverance and commitment to your goals. Breathe deeply and allow the scent to energize you. Use the blend daily or whenever you need a motivational boost. The aromatic qualities will reinforce your resolve and focus.

FAST TRACK ACCELERATOR SPELL JAR FOR MANIFESTATION

MATERIALS

- Incense (optional)
- Pen
- Small piece of paper
- Small glass jar with lid
- A few pieces of citrine
- Ground cinnamon
- A few pieces of clear quartz

1. Find a quiet space where you can focus on your ritual uninterrupted. Cleanse the space and your materials with incense to ensure they are free of any previous energies. Write your goals and intentions on the paper. Fold the paper and place it at the bottom of the jar. This written intention is the foundation of your spell.
2. Next, add a few citrine crystals to the jar, focusing on your desire for these goals to manifest swiftly and positively. Citrine is known for its powerful manifestation properties. Sprinkle a pinch of ground cinnamon over the crystals to symbolize speed and the successful realization of your intentions. Top off the jar with clear quartz crystals to amplify the energy of the citrine and your written intentions.
3. Seal the jar and shake it lightly while visualizing your goals coming to fruition quickly and effectively. Place the jar in a spot where you will see it regularly.
4. Once your goals have manifested, ceremonially open the jar and remove its contents. Thank each element for its assistance in your manifestation journey. You can either cleanse and repurpose the crystals for new projects or carry them with you as a reminder of the abundance in your life.

PHASE 5

THE FULL MOON

CLARITY AND FULFILLMENT

BEST FOR

Manifestation, celebrating milestones, releasing what no longer serves you

The full moon is the pinnacle of the lunar cycle, radiating energy and illumination. This phase is all about manifestation, clarity, and celebrating your progress. The light of the full moon shines on what's been hidden, bringing insights and revelations to the surface. It's a powerful time for completing projects, making important decisions, and acknowledging your achievements. However, the heightened energy can also feel overwhelming, so it's important to stay grounded. Use the full moon to reflect on what has come to fruition and consider what needs to be released to make space for new growth.

PREPARING FOR
THE FULL MOON

As the full moon ascends, it's vital to prepare both your mindset and your environment to fully embrace its illuminating energy. This phase signifies culmination and celebration, making it ideal for reflection and release. Incorporating tools that resonate with the full moon's energy can greatly enhance your ability to capitalize on this phase.

WHAT TO FOCUS ON

DURING THE FULL MOON

Celebrating Progress and Successes

The full moon acts as a spotlight, highlighting the fruits of your labor. Take this time to celebrate your achievements, acknowledge how far you've come, and give gratitude for the blessings you've received along the way.

Letting Go Gracefully

The full moon shines a light on what's hindering your growth, encouraging you to release anything that is no longer serving you—be it old habits, negative thoughts, or unproductive relationships.

Staying Clear and Grounded

The heightened emotions of this phase can be overwhelming, but they also pave the way for breakthroughs. Employ grounding methods such as deep breathing or meditation to maintain balance and access deeper insights.

WHAT TO AVOID

DURING THE FULL MOON

Neglecting to Pause and Reflect

The luminous presence of the full moon can tempt you to make quick decisions. It's wise to pause and reflect, giving yourself space to make well-considered choices rather than reactionary ones.

Stirring Up Conflict

Emotions run high during this time, making it easy to get drawn into unnecessary squabbles. Try to stay calm and collected, avoiding heated discussions or impulsive decisions that you might later regret.

Ignoring Your Intuition

The full moon strengthens your intuitive sense, making it a key source of personal guidance. Ignoring these intuitive nudges and synchronicities can mean missing out on valuable insights intended to steer you in the right direction.

CRYSTALS

Selenite

For clarity and connection to higher wisdom.

Clear Quartz

For amplifying energy and intentions.

Pearl

For purity and the manifestation of true desires.

HERBS AND INCENSE

Jasmine

For introspection and harmony.

Myrrh

For its deep cleansing properties and to facilitate release.

Copal

For connecting to divine energy and spiritual protection.

ITEMS

Symbols of the Harvest

Incorporate items that symbolize the fruits of your labor, such as cornucopias, or bowls filled with fruit. These represent the tangible outcomes and rewards of your hard work.

Reflective Elements

Use items like crystals, water basins, or mirrors that reflect light to symbolize the full moon's power to reveal and clarify.

Divination Tools

Employ tools such as tarot cards, runes, or pendulums to gain insights and guidance. Utilizing these tools can help you tap into the full moon's energy as well as your own intuition for clarity and foresight.

MEDITATION AND VISUALIZATION

Full Moon Meditation for Self-Awareness

Find a quiet place to sit or lie down comfortably. Close your eyes and begin with deep, slow breaths, to ground yourself. Start by bringing your awareness to your feet and slowly work your way through your body. As you scan each area—your legs, hips, torso, arms, shoulders, neck, and head—pay attention to how it feels. Notice any tension, tightness, or areas where emotions feel stored or blocked.

With each exhale, consciously release that tension or emotion, allowing your body to relax more deeply. As you continue this scan, reflect on how certain emotions may manifest physically. Without judgment, simply observe them. End the meditation by taking a few deep breaths, feeling lighter and more in tune with your body.

Full Moon Visualization for Gratitude

In a calm setting, close your eyes and start with purposeful breaths to ground yourself. Visualize a landscape illuminated by the full moon, casting a silvery light over everything. Begin to walk, noticing small objects along the path that represent your successes and milestones.

Pick up these items, examining and acknowledging each one, feeling gratitude for the successes and learning experiences they represent. With each item, feel a sense of joy and appreciation. Reflect on how far you've come and the obstacles you've overcome. After acknowledging each item, place it back down, leaving it behind but carrying the lessons and gratitude forward.

FULL MOON

AFFIRMATIONS

*I am proud of my journey
and how far I've come.*

*I am open to the revelations
and transformations
this full moon brings.*

*I trust that the universe gives
me exactly what I need at
exactly the right time.*

My intuition is always right.

*Being my authentic self
sets my spirit free.*

*I choose to say goodbye
to anything that's holding
me back.*

FULL MOON

RITUALS

As you move from the building energy of the waxing gibbous into the peak of the full moon, you might notice a shift in how you feel—perhaps a bit more on edge or restless. The full moon's energy is at its height, amplifying everything from manifestation and clarity to emotions and inner tension. While this phase is powerful for bringing your intentions to fruition, it can also leave you feeling unbalanced or overwhelmed. If that's the case, remember that it's completely normal. This is a time to make space for all of your emotions, both positive and negative, while staying mindful not to slip into harmful habits or patterns. The following rituals are designed to support you as you navigate this potent lunar energy, allowing you to tap into intentions surrounding abundance, clarity, gratitude, and release.

PROSPERITY SPELL FOR ABUNDANCE

MATERIALS

- Blank check or a piece of paper
- Pen
- Envelope
- Green ribbon or string
- A piece of citrine, pyrite, and green aventurine (optional)

1. Begin by finding a quiet space to set your intention for abundance. Use a blank check if you have one available; otherwise, use a plain piece of paper and mimic the format of a check for symbolic effect. Write the check to yourself, specifying an amount you wish to attract or write "paid in full" to symbolize an abundance covering all your needs.
2. Fold the completed check or paper and place it inside an envelope. Tie a green ribbon or string around it to symbolize growth and prosperity. Enhance the ritual by placing citrine, pyrite, and green aventurine crystals either on top of or inside the envelope to amplify wealth and success.
3. Hold the envelope in your hands, close your eyes, and visualize easily achieving your financial goals. Imagine prosperity flowing towards you and savor the feelings of joy and security that accompany this for a few moments.
4. Choose a significant future date to "cash" your abundance check, such as a birthday, or any date with personal or astrological importance. Write this date on the outside of the envelope as a reminder of when you intend to open it and review your financial manifestations. Store the envelope in a safe place where it can remain undisturbed until then, trusting that the universe will align to fulfill your intentions.

MATERIALS

- Pen and small piece of paper
- Small sachet or cloth pouch
- Dried mugwort, lavender, and chamomile
- Lavender or sandalwood essential oil
- A piece of amethyst
- Dream journal or small notebook

DREAM WEAVER SACHET SPELL FOR INTUITIVE INSIGHTS

1. Begin by writing your specific question or desired insight on a small piece of paper; fold it and set it aside. Take a cloth pouch and gently fill it with a blend of dried mugwort, lavender, and chamomile, each selected for their properties that encourage deep sleep and vivid dreams. Add a few drops of either lavender or sandalwood essential oil to the herbs to enhance relaxation and dream clarity.
2. Place the amethyst inside the sachet to boost intuition and amplify the energy of your intention. Include the folded paper with your question into the sachet, then tie it closed, securing your intentions.
3. Hold the completed sachet in your hands for a few moments, quietly focusing on your question or theme, with the intention of receiving answers from your dreams. At this moment, repeat an affirmation aloud such as, "My dreams always show me what I need to know", to reinforce your intention.
4. Finally, place the sachet under your pillow before going to bed to facilitate a night of insightful dreaming, setting the stage for clarity and revelation as you sleep. Keep a dream journal or small notebook on your nightstand or close to your bed to record your dreams immediately upon waking.

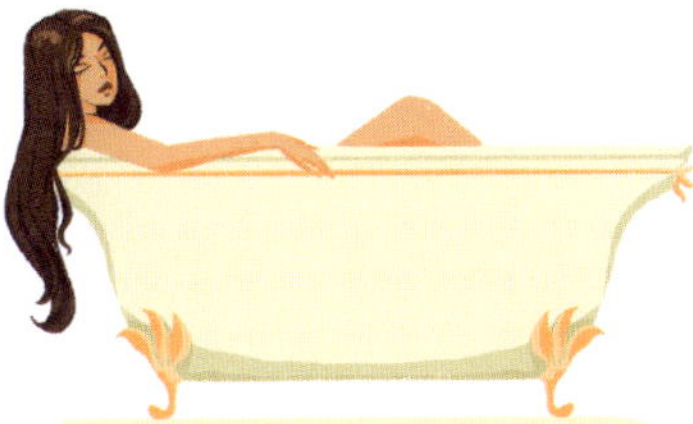

SACRED WATERS RITUAL BATH FOR RELEASE

MATERIALS

- 2 cups (400g) sea salt or Epsom salt
- Lavender and eucalyptus essential oils
- A white or blue candle
- Matches or a lighter
- Small piece of paper and a pen
- A fireproof container

1. Start by filling your bathtub with warm water, then dissolve the sea salt or Epsom salt in the bath, as salt is known for its purifying and cleansing properties.
2. Add a few drops of lavender and eucalyptus essential oils to the water; lavender promotes relaxation and emotional balance, while eucalyptus helps to clear negative energy.
3. Light a white or blue candle near the bathtub for calmness and serenity.
4. Before entering the bath, write down what you wish to release—be it stress or emotional burdens—on a small piece of paper. Fold the paper and hold it over the candle flame carefully, allowing it to burn in the fireproof container. As it burns, visualize the smoke carrying away all that you wish to release.
5. When ready, step into the bath and completely immerse yourself in the soothing water, focusing on the sensation of the salt cleansing and purifying your body and spirit. Allow yourself to feel lighter and freed from the weights you've released as you soak.
6. Once you're finished, step out of the tub. Watch the water flow down the drain, visualizing it carrying away any lingering negative attachments. Conclude the ritual with a deep, mindful breath, then carefully snuff out the candle.

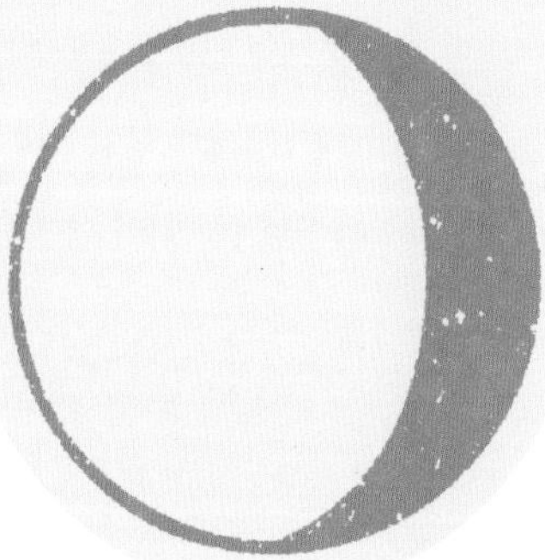

PHASE 6

THE WANING GIBBOUS MOON

GRATITUDE AND SHARING

BEST FOR

Gratitude journaling, sharing experiences or lessons learned, reflecting on recent successes

After the full moon, the waning gibbous phase shifts the focus from action to reflection. The energy begins to wind down, inviting you to look back on what's been accomplished and start processing the lessons learned. This is a time for gratitude, sharing your knowledge, and considering how you can give back. The waning gibbous is ideal for evaluating what worked, what didn't, and how you can carry these insights forward. It's also a great time for mentoring or teaching, as the wisdom you've gained can be valuable to others.

PREPARING FOR
THE WANING GIBBOUS MOON

The waning gibbous phase encourages thoughtful evaluation and the continuation of release processes, making it ideal for deep reflection and fine-tuning your strategies. Integrating tools that resonate with the waning gibbous moon's energy can greatly enhance your ability to engage in these reflective practices.

WHAT TO FOCUS ON

DURING THE WANING GIBBOUS MOON

Sharing Knowledge

Use this phase to mentor others or share your skills. It's a rewarding way to solidify your own understanding while helping others grow and learn from your journey.

Integrating Insights

Reflect on your experiences during the recent full moon and take these lessons to heart. Determining which practices were most effective and identifying areas for improvement can help you better manage your time and resources moving forward.

Cultivating Patience

As the moon wanes, practice patience and understand that not all processes yield immediate results. Focus on the value of gradual progress and the strength found in steady, persistent effort.

WHAT TO AVOID

DURING THE WANING GIBBOUS MOON

Bottling Up Emotions

As you streamline and organize during the waning gibbous, remember to let go of pent-up emotions. Holding on to unresolved feelings can hinder your progress and cloud your clarity.

Forgetting Gratitude

Remember to reflect on what you're grateful for during this lunar phase. Neglecting to acknowledge your gains can stall your emotional growth and diminish the joy of your successes.

Rushing Decision-Making

Avoid the rush to make quick decisions without adequate reflection. The waning gibbous phase encourages thoughtful consideration, especially when integrating new insights or changes.

CRYSTALS

Aquamarine

For letting go and cleansing emotional bodies.

Smoky Quartz

For grounding and releasing negative energy.

Peridot

For alleviating jealousy, resentment, and bitterness.

HERBS AND INCENSE

Chamomile

For relaxation and soothing stress.

Eucalyptus

For healing and renewal.

Lavender

For calming and balancing emotions.

ITEMS

Recycling Bins or Bags

Emphasize the theme of letting go by setting aside items for recycling or donation, clearing out what you no longer need.

Comfort Items

Add cushions, soft blankets, or comfortable seating to your space, encouraging relaxation and reflection after the high energy of the full moon.

Muted Lighting

Opt for softer, dimmer lighting options to match the decreasing light of the moon, creating a calming environment conducive to introspection.

WANING GIBBOUS MOON

MEDITATION AND VISUALIZATION

Waning Gibbous Moon Meditation for Introspection

Find a quiet space and sit comfortably. Close your eyes and take deep breaths to center your thoughts. Visualize the soft light of the waning gibbous moon surrounding you. As you breathe in, draw clarity and peace; as you breathe out, let go of confusion and stagnation.

Ask yourself important reflective questions to guide your thoughts: "What have I learned from my recent experiences?" "What habits or beliefs am I holding that no longer serve me?" "How can I apply the wisdom I've gained to move forward more effectively?" Allow each question to float up naturally and give yourself time to explore the answers deeply. Open your eyes, feeling clear and purposeful.

Waning Gibbous Moon Visualization for Renewal

Sit or lie down in a quiet place, and close your eyes. Take deep breaths to ground yourself in the moment. Envision yourself walking along a tranquil beach lit by the waning gibbous moon. Each step on the cool sand deepens your connection to the earth.

Along your path, find symbolic items like shells or driftwood, each representing outdated thoughts or habits. Pick up each item, recognize its past importance, and gently toss it into the sea. With each item you release, feel lighter and revitalized. After your walk, stand still, absorb the moon's reflective light, and return refreshed, carrying the peace and renewal from your visualization into your daily life.

WANING GIBBOUS MOON

AFFIRMATIONS

I give myself credit for the effort I've put in and the positive changes I've created in my life.

I honor the knowledge I've gathered and feel called to share it in ways that help others grow.

I trust in the lessons life has taught me and use them as tools to keep building my path.

I continue to grow by embracing self-awareness and reflecting on my experiences with honesty and openness.

I free myself from rigid expectations and trust that I can handle whatever comes next.

WANING GIBBOUS MOON

RITUALS

As the moon's light begins to fade, the waning gibbous phase invites you to take a step back, slow down, and turn your attention inward. After the intensity of the full moon, this is your moment to reflect on everything that's surfaced—whether it's a new realization or the results of your efforts. Even as the moon's brightness starts to wane, there's still enough light to help you assess your path with clarity. Did things turn out as you expected, or did they take a different direction? These rituals are here to help you pause, celebrate your wins, and pinpoint areas that might need a little refining. As you move through this phase, it's all about soaking in the lessons and carrying that wisdom with you.

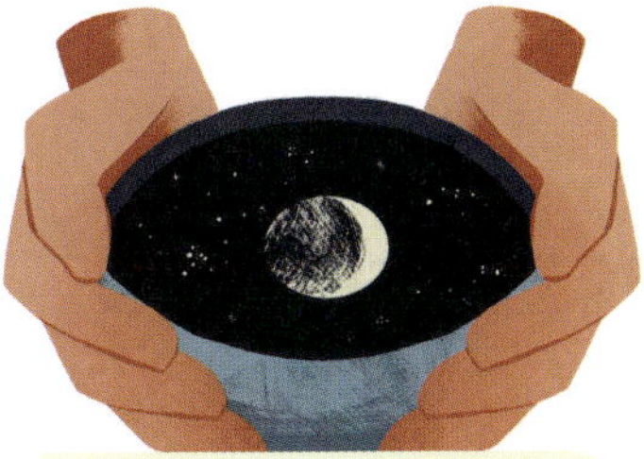

SCRYING RITUAL FOR SELF-REFLECTION

MATERIALS

- Small, dark-colored bowl filled with water or black scrying mirror
- A candle (preferably white or silver)
- Matches or a lighter
- Lavender or sage essential oil
- Journal and pen

1. Begin by setting up a quiet space where you will not be disturbed. Place the bowl of water or black scrying mirror on a flat surface where you can comfortably gaze into it.
2. Light the candle and place it nearby so that it provides light but does not reflect directly in the water or mirror. If using a bowl, add a few drops of lavender or sage essential oil to the water to enhance psychic awareness and calm your mind.
3. Sit comfortably in front of your scrying tool and relax your eyes. Gaze into the surface, letting your vision soften and your mind clear of everyday thoughts. As you enter a meditative state, focus on the themes of the waning gibbous moon: release, introspection, and the wisdom gained from recent experiences. Allow images, colors, or symbols to appear without forcing them, embracing whatever comes with an open mind.
4. Spend a few minutes in this state, or until you feel that the images or insights begin to fade. Gently bring yourself back to your surroundings and snuff out the candle. Immediately record any visions or feelings that came to you during your scrying session in your journal, noting how they might relate to current situations or energies in your life. This practice can reveal deeper subconscious thoughts and highlight areas where release or further reflection is needed.

MATERIALS

- A sturdy ruler or straight-edged book
- 2 small stones or coins (or 1 light and 1 dark crystal, such as selenite and obsidian)
- A white candle
- Matches or a lighter

BALANCE BEAM SPELL FOR HARMONY

1. Begin by finding a quiet space where you can set up your materials without disturbance. Place the ruler or straight-edged book on a flat surface, creating your "balance beam". Select your balancing items: either two small stones or coins, or one light and one dark crystal like selenite and obsidian to represent the balance of opposing energies. Place each stone, coin, or crystal at opposite ends of the ruler or book, ensuring they stay balanced.
2. Next, light the white candle and place it in a safe position near the center of your balance beam. Allow your gaze to settle on the candle's flame. Begin to think about the areas of your life that feel imbalanced. Consider any aspects of your life that have excess energy or focus, as well as those that have been neglected. Once these areas are clear in your mind, visualize bringing them into alignment, harmonizing them until they come into balance, just like the objects on the balance beam before you.
3. As you hold this vision, feel the sense of equilibrium growing stronger within you. When you're ready, gently snuff out the candle, symbolizing your intention to carry this newfound balance into your daily life. Keep the balance beam setup in a place where you can see it daily as a reminder of your commitment to maintaining harmony.

UNITY BRAID RITUAL FOR COLLECTIVE WISDOM

MATERIALS

- 3 different colored ribbons or strands of yarn

1. Begin by selecting three ribbons or strands of yarn, each in a color that represents a specific lesson you've recently learned—perhaps one for personal growth, another for relationships, and a third for career or life purpose. Find a quiet space where you can focus on your intentions.
2. Hold the three strands in your hands, taking a moment to reflect on the lessons each one symbolizes. Tie the strands into a knot at one end, then begin to braid them. As you weave, imagine the different aspects of your wisdom coming together, forming a unified cord. Acknowledge the growth you've achieved in these areas.
3. Visualize this wisdom becoming more potent and cohesive. Once the braid is complete, tie the two ends together to form a circle, symbolizing the unity and interconnectedness of all wisdom, as well as the collective nature of shared knowledge. Hold the finished braid, feeling the power of the threads you've woven and the progress they represent.
4. Place this circular braid in a special place in your home, or carry it with you as a reminder to share these lessons with others. Let this unbroken circle inspire you to contribute your insights to the greater collective, fostering connection and growth for all.

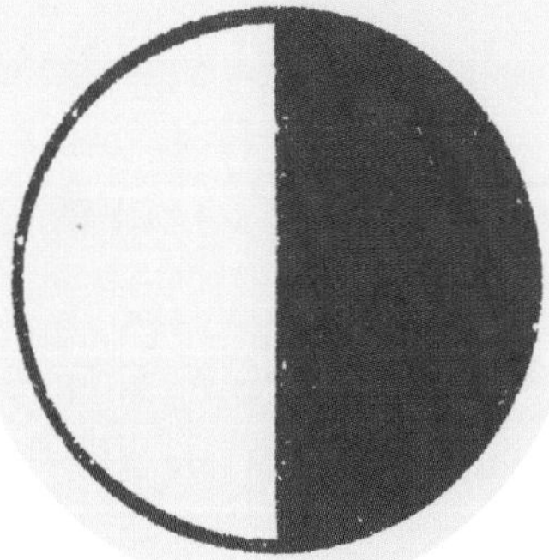

PHASE 7

THE THIRD QUARTER MOON

RELEASE AND LETTING GO

BEST FOR

Releasing emotional baggage, forgiveness exercises, identifying and letting go of limiting beliefs, shadow work practices

The third quarter moon, also referred to as the last quarter moon, is a phase of introspection and release. It's a time to confront any lingering obstacles or patterns that might be holding you back. The energy here encourages you to take responsibility for your actions, embrace forgiveness, and tie up any loose ends. This phase is somewhat of a final call for closure, allowing you to make peace with the past before the lunar cycle comes to a close. Use the third quarter phase to clear out what no longer serves you and prepare for the renewal that's just around the corner.

PREPARING FOR
THE THIRD QUARTER MOON

As the third quarter moon invites you to critically assess and let go of what no longer serves your growth, it's essential to cultivate an environment of calm and clarity. Choose a peaceful setting that minimizes distractions – a quiet room, a secluded spot in nature or any place where you feel grounded and undisturbed. Prepare yourself mentally by adopting an open and willing attitude to embrace change and detachment, setting the stage for transformative experiences during this introspective phase.

WHAT TO FOCUS ON

DURING THE THIRD QUARTER MOON

Owning Your Actions

As the moon wanes, it's a potent time to reflect on your contributions to your life's path. This phase is about cultivating self-awareness and taking responsibility for your decisions so you can continue to evolve.

Embracing Forgiveness

Use the energy of release associated with this moon phase to forgive yourself and others. Clearing old grievances and letting go of emotional baggage allows you to make room for new growth.

Finding Your Equilibrium

This half-illuminated phase invites you to cultivate balance in your life. Evaluate where you may be overextending or neglecting aspects to enhance overall harmony.

WHAT TO AVOID

DURING THE THIRD QUARTER MOON

Dwelling on Past Failures

Instead of ruminating on what didn't work out, use lessons learned to improve future actions. Accepting your own flaws and treating yourself with kindness and compassion is also important. Remember, everyone makes mistakes!

Holding on to Grudges

Don't let resentment hold you back. During the third quarter moon, take the time to recognize and honor these emotions, then actively release them in a healthy way, such as through art or writing.

Resisting Closure

Avoid the temptation to cling to past situations, relationships, or emotions that are nearing their natural end. This phase is a prime time for letting go and moving on. Resisting closure can keep you stuck in repetitive patterns and prevent the necessary space for new growth and opportunities.

CRYSTALS

Obsidian

For illuminating and releasing lingering energetic attachments.

Hematite

For grounding and absorbing negativity.

Howlite

For patience and self-awareness.

HERBS AND INCENSE

Thyme

For releasing the past and overcoming grief.

Cedar

For cleansing and maintaining balance.

Patchouli

For grounding and stimulating the release of emotional barriers.

ITEMS

Symbols of Release

Incorporate items that represent letting go, such as feathers or old leaves, symbolizing the shedding of past layers and unnecessary burdens.

Restorative Items

Include yoga mats, meditation cushions, or sound healing instruments like singing bowls to support inward focus and spiritual realignment.

Earthy Tones

Decorate with colors and materials that ground you to nature, such as browns and greens, terracotta pots, or wooden elements, aiding in grounding and centering energies.

MEDITATION AND VISUALIZATION

Third Quarter Moon Meditation for Clarity

Find a quiet space to sit. Begin by focusing on deep, steady breaths, inhaling clarity and exhaling tension. Once you feel centered, clear your mind and shift your attention to any mental or emotional blocks that are holding you back. Without forcing anything, allow the first words or thoughts that pop into your mind to surface. Don't judge them—just observe. These words may point toward deeper obstacles.

As each thought arises, breathe deeply and visualize releasing it with your exhale. After a few minutes, notice if any patterns emerge. Once you've finished, reflect on these insights and journal about what came up. This practice encourages clarity by helping you identify hidden subconscious blocks from an objective point of view.

Third Quarter Moon Visualization for Release

Close your eyes and imagine yourself as a strong, towering tree in the middle of fall. Feel your roots providing stability. Your branches are full of leaves, each leaf represents an unresolved emotion or a lingering conflict. As you breathe, a gentle breeze begins to blow.

With each exhale, the wind pulls the leaves from your branches, allowing them to float to the ground. As each leaf falls, you feel lighter, more open, and free. You recognize that by letting go, you are making room for new growth and possibilities in the seasons to come. Feel the lightness within, knowing you are ready to move forward.

THIRD QUARTER MOON

AFFIRMATIONS

I forgive myself and others, knowing that holding on to the past only weighs me down.

I take responsibility for my actions and understand the impact of my choices.

I accept my past mistakes as valuable lessons and move forward with wisdom.

My spirit is resilient and adaptable in the face of change.

I am fully aware of the patterns and habits that no longer serve me and choose to release them.

I accept myself unconditionally, flaws and all.

THIRD QUARTER MOON

RITUALS

Sometimes, the biggest obstacle to our growth is ourselves. When we experience hurt or disappointment, we tend to hold on to anger, resentment, or regret, thinking that we're protecting ourselves by doing so. But in reality, clinging to these negative emotions only weighs us down and keeps us from moving forward. The third quarter moon invites us to confront this pattern, offering us the opportunity to release these emotional burdens once and for all. By leaning into the energy of release that this phase brings, we can make conscious decisions to let go of what no longer serves us—whether that's a lingering grudge, past regrets, or self-imposed limitations. The rituals in this section are here to support you in that process, helping you clear the way for peace, healing, and a renewed sense of freedom.

GOODBYE BAGGAGE WRITING RITUAL FOR CLOSURE

MATERIALS

- A journal or sheet of paper
- A piece of blue sodalite
- Pen

1. Begin by finding a quiet space where you can focus. Sit comfortably with your journal and hold the blue sodalite in your hands. Close your eyes, take a few deep breaths, and allow the crystal's calming energy to help you open up and express your emotions more clearly.
2. Focus on the emotional baggage you want to release as you hold the crystal. Feel the weight of these emotions and allow them to rise to the surface. Place the crystal beside you or keep it in your non-writing hand to continue supporting clear, honest communication.
3. Begin writing a letter to yourself or to the person or situation that you feel has caused you emotional pain. Pour out all your thoughts and feelings, letting the words flow without judgment. Be as honest as possible, knowing that this writing is for your healing alone.
4. Once you have expressed everything you need to, hold the crystal again, and reaffirm your intention to let go of the emotional baggage you've been holding on to by repeating the affirmation, "I release these words and the weight they carry." If you're ready, you can burn the letter safely or tear it up, symbolizing the final act of letting go. End the ritual by placing the blue sodalite on your heart or throat for a few moments, feeling the peace of release.

PEACE-WITH-THE-PAST KNOT SPELL FOR FORGIVENESS

MATERIALS

- A length of string or cord (something thick that you can untie, like a shoelace)

1. Begin by finding a quiet space where you can focus without distractions. Hold the string or cord in your hands, and take a few deep breaths to center yourself. As you inhale, think about the person, situation, or aspect of yourself that you need to forgive. With each exhale, feel the tension and unresolved emotions rise to the surface.
2. Begin tying knots in the string, one for each hurt, grievance, or negative emotion you've been holding on to. As you tie each knot, acknowledge the pain or resentment associated with it. Say aloud or silently, "I acknowledge this pain, and I am ready to release it."
3. Once all the knots are tied, hold the cord and speak your intention for forgiveness: "I release these hurts and forgive for the sake of my own peace." Visualize the knots absorbing the negative emotions and energy.
4. Next, begin to untie each knot slowly, imagining the pain and resentment unraveling with each one. Feel the weight lifting as you undo each knot. Once all the knots are untied, bury or discard the string, symbolizing the final release. Close the ritual by taking a deep breath, feeling lighter and more at peace.

STONE OF STABILITY SPELL FOR GROUNDING

MATERIALS

- A grounding stone (such as hematite, black tourmaline, or smoky quartz)

1. Begin by finding a quiet, undisturbed space to sit comfortably, ideally outside, where you can stand barefoot. Hold your chosen grounding stone in your hands, feeling its weight and texture. Close your eyes, take a few deep breaths, and allow yourself to connect with the Earth's energy through the stone.
2. As you hold the stone, focus on your intention to remain grounded and stable, no matter what challenges or uncertainties arise. Visualize roots growing from the soles of your feet, extending deep into the Earth, anchoring you firmly. Feel the stone's energy reinforcing this connection, making you feel secure and balanced.
3. When you're ready, speak your intention: "I am rooted in the Earth, stable and secure. This stone anchors me in strength and balance." Imagine the stone absorbing this intention, becoming a powerful talisman of grounding.
4. Carry the stone with you throughout the day, keeping it in your pocket or bag, or place it on your desk or bedside table as a constant reminder of your stability and connection to the Earth. Hold the stone again and reaffirm your grounding whenever you feel unsteady, allowing its energy to restore your balance and peace.

PHASE 8

THE WANING CRESCENT MOON

SURRENDER AND REST

BEST FOR

Rest and recovery, meditation, solitary practices, deep introspection

As the lunar cycle draws to a close, the waning crescent moon offers a moment of deep rest and surrender. The energy here is quiet and introspective, encouraging you to slow down, let go, and reflect on the journey you've just completed. This is a time for healing, self-care, and embracing stillness. With the light of the moon nearly gone, the waning crescent invites you to find peace in the darkness, trusting that the next new moon will bring a fresh start. It's a phase for turning inward, releasing any lingering attachments, and preparing your spirit for renewal.

PREPARING FOR
THE WANING CRESCENT MOON

As the waning crescent moon approaches, it's the perfect time to wind down and prepare for renewal. Physically declutter your space and consider a gentle detox to clear your body. Energetically, practice stillness and deep reflection. Embrace a mindset of letting go and connecting with your intuition, allowing yourself to receive fresh insights and energy.

WHAT TO FOCUS ON

DURING THE WANING CRESCENT MOON

Deepening Introspection

The waning crescent moon is the perfect time for deep introspection. Use meditation or journaling to explore your inner thoughts and reflect on your entire journey throughout the lunar cycle.

Cleansing Your Space

Physically clear your environment of clutter and symbolically remove old energies. This could involve smoke cleansing with incense or simply deep cleaning your living space.

Prioritizing Rest

Allow yourself more rest than usual during this quiet moon phase. Sleep and relaxation are vital for resetting your energy levels in preparation for the new moon.

WHAT TO AVOID

DURING THE WANING CRESCENT MOON

Forcing Outcomes

During this phase, resist the urge to force resolutions or hurry outcomes. The waning crescent moon encourages letting things unfold naturally, allowing space for organic conclusions and transitions.

Indulging in Vices

Avoid letting vices take the wheel during this introspective phase. Activities that overstimulate or unbalance you can detract from the valuable personal discoveries that this time can foster.

Overextending Yourself

Take care not to stretch yourself too thin during this time. This phase calls for conserving your energy and preparing for renewal. Overcommitting, whether socially or at work, can leave you drained and less prepared for the new lunar cycle.

CRYSTALS

Amethyst

For enhancing spiritual awareness and intuition.

Lepidolite

For transition and stress relief.

Angelite

For rest and surrendering to the universe.

HERBS AND INCENSE

Garden Sage

For wisdom and clearing out negativity.

Yarrow

For healing and protection.

Juniper

For cleansing and inner peace.

ITEMS

Symbols of Closure

Incorporating symbols that represent closure can enhance your connection to this phase. Use items like a knotted rope to symbolize the tying up of loose ends, or a lock to represent securing past lessons.

Purifying Elements

Utilizing elements that purify your space can help clear out old energies. Items like salt can be used to create protective boundaries or cleanse crystals, and water, ideal for ritual baths, to remove negativity.

Diaries or Dream Journals

Place journals prominently to encourage the recording of dreams, reflections, or any other insights that arise as this final phase comes to a close.

WANING CRESCENT MOON

MEDITATION AND VISUALIZATION

Waning Crescent Moon Meditation for Surrender

Find a serene place to sit or lie down comfortably. Close your eyes and deepen your breathing to establish a state of deep relaxation and receptivity. Visualize the slender waning crescent moon, its faint light a symbol of the waning cycle of your own experiences. As you breathe, imagine each exhale as an opportunity to release worries, regrets, and all forms of mental clutter. Ask yourself: "What can I release to make space for new beginnings?" Let this meditation deepen your sense of surrender, easing the transition to the next cycle. After several minutes, open your eyes, feeling unburdened and refreshed.

Waning Crescent Moon Visualization for Inner Peace

Choose a quiet and comfortable spot to begin this visualization. Imagine yourself sitting by a calm, reflective pool under the night sky, illuminated by the waning crescent moon. Each ripple on the water's surface represents a thought or feeling you are letting go of. Watch these ripples slowly fade away, leaving the water smooth and undisturbed. Feel this stillness reflect in your own mind, creating a deep sense of peace and readiness for the new cycle. Conclude this visualization with a few deep, calming breaths, and when you feel complete, gently open your eyes, carrying with you the tranquility of the scene.

WANING CRESCENT MOON

AFFIRMATIONS

It's okay to rest; my energy will return when the time is right.

I allow myself to slow down and trust the process unfolding before me.

I am healing at my own pace and in my own unique way.

I honor the quiet moments as sacred space for healing and renewal.

I let go of striving and allow myself to simply be in this moment.

WANING CRESCENT MOON

RITUALS

As your journey through the lunar cycle nears its end with the waning crescent moon, it's the perfect time to slow down and embrace rest. Energy levels may naturally be lower during this phase, which can make it tempting to skip out on rituals altogether, but don't underestimate the power of this phase! While the waning crescent might seem quiet or uneventful, remember that there's a lot happening beneath the surface. You might feel as if you're not doing much when in reality, your subconscious is actively processing, healing, and preparing for the new cycle ahead. These carefully curated rituals are crafted to guide you through this introspective stage, helping you recharge and align as you prepare for the new moon's arrival.

MATERIALS

- A pot of water
- 1 lemon, sliced
- 1 handful of fresh rosemary
- 1 cinnamon stick
- 3 bay leaves
- 2–3 cloves

SIMMER POT RITUAL FOR DEEP CLEANSING

1. Set your intention to purify your home and aura in preparation for the new lunar cycle. Fill a pot with water and place it on the stove over medium heat. As the water warms, add the lemon slices, envisioning them bringing clarity and freshness into your space.
2. Next, add the rosemary, focusing on its protective and purifying properties. Drop in the cinnamon stick, allowing its warmth to infuse your home with positive energy. Add the bay leaves, thinking about the wisdom and renewal you wish to invite into the upcoming cycle. Finally, add the cloves, imagining them banishing any lingering negativity.
3. Bring the mixture to a gentle simmer, then reduce the heat to low and let it simmer for 1–2 hours, allowing the cleansing steam to fill your space. As the aroma circulates, take deep breaths, visualizing your home and aura being purified.
4. When finished, let the pot cool, then strain the liquid and use it to wipe down doorways or windowsills, sealing in its cleansing effect. The remaining solids can be composted or scattered in your garden, symbolizing renewal and the return of positive energy to the earth.

SOUND BATH RITUAL FOR SURRENDERING CONTROL

MATERIALS

- Comfortable mat or blanket
- Candles or incense for ambiance (optional)
- Cushion or pillow
- Singing bowls, tuning forks, or recorded sound bath tracks

1. Place a comfortable mat or blanket on the floor, and if desired, enhance the atmosphere with candles or incense. Settle yourself on the mat or blanket, using a cushion or pillow for support.
2. Start by taking deep, centering breaths, focusing your intention on releasing your need for control and trusting the universe's plan. If you're using singing bowls or tuning forks, begin to play them gently. Alternatively, if you prefer recorded tracks, set up your device to play a sound bath session. Close your eyes and let the sound envelop you, whether live or recorded, allowing the vibrations to resonate deeply within.
3. Visualize the sounds as waves of light washing over you, clearing away all tensions and worries. Imagine any barriers or resistance dissolving, guiding you into a state of complete surrender. Continue engaging with the sounds as long as feels right, letting them lead you into deeper relaxation and trust.
4. When you feel ready, gradually reduce the volume or stop playing the instruments. Remain seated or lying down for a few moments to internalize the peaceful state you've achieved. Acknowledge the renewed sense of trust and release. Open your eyes, bringing this serenity into your everyday life.

BUILDING A COSMIC CONNECTION ALTAR

MATERIALS

- A small table or shelf for setup
- Incense
- Matches or a lighter
- A blue or purple cloth
- Feathers
- Coins
- Blue crystals (such as sodalite or lapis lazuli)
- Symbols of trust (such as keys, rings, or knotted rope)

1. Begin by selecting a quiet corner of your room to build your altar. Start by cleansing the area with incense, allowing the smoke to clear away negative energy.
2. Lay down a blue or purple cloth to set the foundation of your altar—these colors soothe the spirit and represent trust and wisdom. Arrange feathers to symbolize your spiritual journey and elevated consciousness. Intersperse coins among the feathers to invite abundance and trust in the universe's generosity.
3. Place blue crystals like sodalite or lapis lazuli strategically around the altar. These stones are known for enhancing intuition and helping you connect with your inner truth. Add personal symbols of trust that resonate with you, or rings, keys, or knotted rope to strengthen your connection to the cosmos.
4. As you set up each item, focus on your intention to open up your aspirations and fears to the universe. Feel each object's placement reinforcing this bond. Once your altar is arranged, spend a few moments at it each day reflecting on the lessons you've learned during this lunar cycle. This daily practice will deepen your connection with the universal energies that guide you. Remember, this altar is a living space that evolves with your spiritual journey, so feel free to add or rearrange elements as your relationship with the universe grows.

CHAPTER
5

THE MOON IN ASTROLOGY

In astrology, the moon plays a key role, deeply influencing our emotions, instincts, and the subtle workings of our subconscious. While the sun highlights our identity and purpose, the moon delves into our innermost feelings, shaping how we react and what makes us feel safe and secure. It impacts our daily life in various ways, from shifting our moods to uncovering our natural tendencies to nurture and care. Each aspect reveals a little more about who we are beneath the surface. In this chapter, we'll look at how the moon affects us in two important ways: by its movement through the zodiac and through the personal meanings of our moon signs.

THE MOON'S TRANSITS THROUGH THE ZODIAC SIGNS

The sun spends about a month in each zodiac sign, creating what we call a 'zodiac season'. This is a time when the qualities of that sign influence our general atmosphere—like a backdrop to a stage play. During each sign's season, we might find ourselves drawn to activities that align with that sign's strengths—like initiating new projects during pioneering Aries season or fostering partnerships during diplomatic Libra season.

The moon , however, travels through each zodiac sign approximately every two and a half days, completing a full cycle through all twelve signs in about twenty-eight days. As it moves, it carries distinct energies that influence our emotions, instincts, and daily behaviors. By understanding these lunar transits, you can better align your actions and intentions with the moon's current energy. This guide will tell you what to expect as the moon passes through each sign and provide insights for maximizing the potential of each new moon and full moon, along with a quick practical tip to support you each step of the way.

♈

MOON IN ARIES

BEST FOR | Starting projects, engaging in high-intensity exercise or competitive sports, going on a first date, searching or applying for new jobs, taking risks, and tackling challenges head-on.

WATCH OUT FOR | Impulsiveness and impatience, which can lead to hasty decisions or conflicts. Be mindful of acting too quickly without fully considering the consequences or the feelings of others.

When the moon is in Aries, you may feel a surge of energy, enthusiasm, and a desire for action. This transit encourages spontaneity, courage, and a pioneering spirit. As the first sign of the zodiac, Aries is all about initiation, so channel your inner warrior and move forward with confidence.

NEW MOON IN ARIES | Focus on setting bold, new intentions that embrace courage and independence, taking the initiative to start fresh projects or pursue personal goals that light you up and make you feel inspired.

FULL MOON IN ARIES | Focus on asserting yourself and taking decisive action. Realize where you need to be more direct and don't be afraid to put yourself first or stand up for what you believe in. At the same time, be cognizant of others' needs by tempering your drive with a generous dose of patience and understanding.

PRACTICAL TIPS | Adding coffee grounds to spells and rituals during this time may help to "speed" up their effect and allow you to achieve your goals more quickly. If you get restless or impatient, don't lash out—instead, choose a physical outlet to blow off steam. Bonus points if it's something out of your comfort zone or gets your adrenaline pumping, like kickboxing, paintballing, or axe throwing.

♉

MOON IN TAURUS

BEST FOR | Enjoying life's sensual pleasures, long-term financial planning, listening to music, visiting an art gallery, getting out in nature, grounding rituals, napping, and treating yourself to a fancy meal.

WATCH OUT FOR | Stubbornness and resistance to change, which can prevent you from adapting to new opportunities or perspectives. Be cautious of clinging too tightly to your comfort zone.

When the moon is in Taurus, you're likely to feel a strong desire for comfort, security, and grounding. This transit encourages you to slow down, appreciate the finer things in life, and focus on building lasting stability. As an Earth sign ruled by Venus, Taurus is all about creating and enjoying beauty, whether in your environment, relationships, or personal achievements.

NEW MOON IN TAURUS | Focus on starting projects that require patience and perseverance, such as saving for a big purchase, setting intentions related to financial growth, or creating a comfortable and secure home environment.

FULL MOON IN TAURUS | This is a time to appreciate what you've achieved and revel in the security and comfort it brings. Stay present and immerse yourself in the now through your senses. Consider what truly matters and let go of any material possessions that aren't enriching your life. Use this moment to focus on your inner abundance rather than external attachment.

PRACTICAL TIPS | Keeping a jar or piggy bank for loose change near your front door can encourage the habit of saving and serve as a tangible reminder of your financial security. Alternatively, setting up an automatic monthly transfer of a small sum of money from your checking to a savings account can achieve the same effect (if you already do this, consider bumping up the amount). If you don't have a savings account yet, make a commitment to research your options during this time and discuss setting one up with your bank.

♊

MOON IN GEMINI

BEST FOR | Engaging in social activities, networking, learning new skills, brainstorming ideas, multitasking, writing, taking short trips, and exploring new interests.

WATCH OUT FOR | Scattered energy and overthinking, which can lead to feeling overwhelmed or indecisive. Be mindful of trying to do too many things at once without clear focus.

When the moon is in Gemini, your mind may feel more active, curious, and adaptable. This transit centers around themes of communication, versatility, and a desire for mental stimulation. As an air sign ruled by Mercury, Gemini energy is light, quick, and changeable, making it an excellent time for gathering information, connecting with others, and multitasking.

NEW MOON IN GEMINI | Be open to trying new things and meeting new people, whether that means signing up for a cooking class, joining a book club, or learning more about a subject you're interested in. Nurture your curiosities and set intentions for personal growth and self-expression.

FULL MOON IN GEMINI | Take this time to sharpen your communication. Are your words opening doors and deepening connections? Reflect on the effectiveness of your dialogue in achieving your goals. You might need to let go of old communication habits that are holding you back.

PRACTICAL TIPS | Setting limits for screen time or social media usage on your phone can help curb distractions and prevent overstimulation during this period. Assess which apps you use the most and set daily time limits for them if the option is available. You can also choose to start out with a simpler goal, such as not using your phone 1–2 hours before bedtime.

♋

MOON IN CANCER

BEST FOR | Spending time at home with close friends or family, nurturing relationships, getting in touch with your roots, communicating with ancestors, connecting with your emotions, cooking nourishing foods, honing your intuition, and creating a safe and cozy environment.

WATCH OUT FOR | Oversensitivity and retreating too much into your shell. Be cautious of becoming overly defensive or withdrawing from those who care about you.

When the moon is in Cancer, emotions tend to run deep, and there's a heightened focus on matters of the heart and home. This transit encourages you to turn inward, prioritize your emotional well-being, and create a nurturing space for yourself and those you care about. As a water sign ruled by the moon itself, Cancer's energy is intuitive, protective, and tender.

NEW MOON IN CANCER | Make space to honor your emotions by engaging in self-care practices. Remember, your sensitivity is your superpower! Allow your feelings to guide and inform your intentions for emotional well-being.

FULL MOON IN CANCER | Reflect on what makes you feel secure and cared for and whether your emotional needs are being met. Focus on releasing any past hurts or unresolved feelings that may be holding you back.

PRACTICAL TIPS | Carrying a reusable water bottle with you throughout the day is an easy way to stay on top of your hydration goals. Since Cancer rules the stomach and water is essential for nourishing our bodies, consuming more of it—whether through comforting foods or drinks like soups, stews, or smoothies—can be beneficial. Choose healthy ingredients that promote gut health, such as ones with fiber or probiotics, if easily tolerated.

♌

MOON IN LEO

BEST FOR | Dressing to impress, grand romantic gestures, entertaining friends, celebrating achievements, embracing your leadership abilities, hosting parties, nurturing your inner child, and seeking recognition.

WATCH OUT FOR | Pride and the need for validation, which can lead to overextending yourself or seeking approval from others. There's a tendency to take things personally during this time, so be mindful of stirring up drama.

When the moon is in Leo, there's an emphasis on self-expression, creativity, and sparking joy. This is a time to let your unique light shine and indulge in activities that make you feel alive and inspired. Leo, ruled by the sun, brings warmth, charisma, and a desire for recognition, making it a great time to showcase your talents or take the lead at work.

NEW MOON IN LEO | Prioritize your passions and listen to your heart's desires. Set intentions for showing up as your most authentic self and being bold in the pursuit of love or self-expression.

FULL MOON IN LEO | Focus on celebrating your achievements and stepping into the spotlight. Take a moment to consider whether you're fully sharing your unique gifts with the world or holding back. It's time to release any insecurities that keep you from being seen.

PRACTICAL TIPS |
Begin each morning by polishing your appearance with a personal touch. It doesn't take much—a quick swipe of bold lipstick, a new hairstyle, or a spritz of your favorite perfume can be a simple yet powerful expression of self-love. After you've finished, take a moment to look in the mirror, repeat a positive affirmation, and carry that confident energy with you all day. Adding a piece of gold jewelry can also enhance this ritual by linking you to the sun's radiant energy and inviting abundance into your life.

♍

MOON IN VIRGO

BEST FOR | Organizing and decluttering your space, prioritizing health, detail-oriented tasks, practical problem solving, cleansing rituals, refining routines, and self-improvement.

WATCH OUT FOR | Perfectionism and self-criticism, which can lead to unnecessary stress or frustration. Be cautious of being too hard on yourself or others in the pursuit of excellence.

When the moon is in Virgo, it brings a grounded, detail-oriented energy that encourages us to focus on organization and practical matters. This is a great time to tackle tasks requiring precision and attention to detail, like cleaning, planning, or getting your health routines in order. Virgo's energy promotes clarity and creates structure, making it easier to bring balance and order to your life.

NEW MOON IN VIRGO | Create goals related to refining your routines, building better habits, and improving productivity. It's an ideal time to clear out clutter and start fresh.

FULL MOON IN VIRGO | Focus on evaluating your progress and ways to improve while practicing self-compassion. Release attachments to certain outcomes and recognize that perfection isn't always attainable.

PRACTICAL TIPS | When starting a new habit, keep it simple at first. Begin with something manageable, like drinking a glass of water first thing in the morning or taking a quick stroll around the block. Stick with these basics for several weeks until they become a regular part of your routine, then gradually introduce more challenging goals. Remember, it's a slow process, so be patient—it often takes a while to notice the effects of these changes.

Ω

MOON IN LIBRA

BEST FOR | Cultivating harmony and balance, strengthening one-to-one relationships, negotiating contracts, seeking justice, elevating aesthetics, and engaging in creative collaborations.

WATCH OUT FOR | Indecisiveness and people-pleasing, which can lead to difficulty making choices or neglecting your own needs. Be mindful of maintaining your own boundaries while striving for harmony with others.

When the moon is in Libra, there's a strong emphasis on bringing balance to our lives. This transit encourages you to focus on your relationships, whether it's spending quality time with loved ones, resolving conflicts, or working collaboratively with others. Libra, ruled by Venus, brings an appreciation for beauty and aesthetics, making it a wonderful time to feed your artistic inclinations.

NEW MOON IN LIBRA | This is a great time to kick-start new relationships and strengthen partnerships. Set your sights on nurturing connections rooted in fairness and mutual respect, whether personal or professional.

FULL MOON IN LIBRA | Take this time to evaluate the balance in your relationships. Think about whether you're giving too much or perhaps not enough and make adjustments to establish a healthier dynamic. Don't compromise your own well-being just to avoid conflict.

PRACTICAL TIPS | Enhance your love spells by adding a pinch of sugar or a drizzle of honey to "sweeten" the outcomes. These ingredients are excellent for drawing in blessings and fostering kindness and affection in your relationships, whether new or established. Sugar quickly attracts positive attention and dissolves obstacles, while honey is great for sealing intentions and nurturing long-term bonds.

♏

MOON IN SCORPIO

BEST FOR | Shadow work, exploring spirituality or the occult, engaging in research or investigative work, reading between the lines, trusting your gut instincts, enhancing intimacy, and strategizing.

WATCH OUT FOR | Obsessiveness and holding on to grudges, which can lead to emotional intensity that's difficult to manage. Be cautious of becoming overly fixated on control or getting stuck in negative emotions.

When the moon is in Scorpio, emotions run deep, and there's a strong pull toward introspection and transformation. This transit encourages intense focus, uncovering hidden truths, and embracing change. Scorpio's energy is passionate and determined, making it an ideal time to dive into emotional healing, explore your inner depths, or engage in transformative practices.

NEW MOON IN SCORPIO | Focus on setting intentions around personal empowerment and shedding any lingering attachments or fears. This is the perfect time for shadow work, journaling, or

intention-setting rituals that encourage deep emotional release and the reclaiming of your inner strength.

FULL MOON IN SCORPIO | Focus on embracing emotional intensity and bringing hidden feelings or unresolved issues to the surface for closure. This is a time for purging anything that feels stagnant, whether through cathartic release rituals, energetic cleansing, or cutting ties with toxic influences in your life.

PRACTICAL TIPS | Wearing or keeping a black crystal on your body, such as obsidian, onyx, or black tourmaline, can help you stay grounded and safe during emotionally turbulent times. In color magic, black is associated with protection and banishing, so carrying black crystals can support you in navigating uncomfortable truths or challenges without fear.

MOON IN SAGITTARIUS

BEST FOR | Seeking adventure, expanding your knowledge, spontaneous travel, engaging in philosophical discussions, learning new skills, attracting luck, and breaking away from routines.

WATCH OUT FOR | Over-commitment, recklessness, or restlessness that can lead to scattered energy and impulsive decisions. Be cautious of neglecting responsibilities in favor of pursuing fun or excitement.

When the moon is in Sagittarius, the energy is light, adventurous, and optimistic. This is a great time for stepping outside of your comfort zone, seeking new experiences, and feeding your curiosity. Sagittarius encourages exploration, whether that's through travel, learning something new, or expanding your horizons in a way that brings personal growth and excitement.

NEW MOON IN SAGITTARIUS | Focus on setting intentions around adventure, growth, and expanding your mind. This is a perfect time to plan future travels, enroll in a course, or set goals for broadening your perspective through reading or learning.

FULL MOON IN SAGITTARIUS | Take stock of your growth and the wisdom you've accrued. Use this moment to identify and let go of outdated beliefs that put a limit on your sense of freedom. While you aim for the stars, remember to ground your dreams with practical plans.

PRACTICAL TIPS | Prioritize trying new things and expanding your horizons. Whether it's booking plane tickets for a future trip, buying concert tickets, making a reservation at a new restaurant, or simply exploring a different neighborhood near you, these new experiences can invigorate your spirit. A change of scenery helps prevent stagnation, so embrace the adventure, no matter how big or small.

♑

MOON IN CAPRICORN

BEST FOR | Planning long-term goals, focusing on career and ambition, structuring your routines, improving discipline, and making practical decisions.

WATCH OUT FOR | Overworking or becoming too rigid in your thinking, which can lead to burnout or a lack of flexibility. Be cautious of being too hard on yourself or others, as Capricorn's influence can amplify perfectionism and self-criticism.

When the moon is in Capricorn, the energy shifts towards practicality, discipline, and ambition. This is an ideal time to focus on your long-term goals and get organized in both your personal and professional life. Capricorn encourages hard work and determination, making this phase great for making concrete plans, tackling tasks with patience, and setting yourself up for future success.

NEW MOON IN CAPRICORN | Focus on setting intentions around career, stability, and long-term success. This is a great time to set practical goals, create a step-by-step plan for achieving them, and commit to building a solid foundation for your future. Use this energy to get clear on what you want to accomplish and take the first steps towards it with discipline and focus.

FULL MOON IN CAPRICORN | Focus on balancing your ambitions with emotional well-being. Celebrate your achievements, but also assess whether your drive for success has left your emotional needs neglected. Capricorn's energy can push you toward overwork, so use this time to release workaholic tendencies and create space for rest, connection, and emotional fulfillment.

PRACTICAL TIPS | Beat procrastination by zeroing in on one key task each day. Tackling the most important job first can prevent the stress of piling responsibilities. This approach enables steady progress and build a sense of achievement without feeling swamped.

MOON IN AQUARIUS

BEST FOR | Embracing innovation, exploring new ideas, connecting with like-minded people, volunteering, organizing community events, challenging the status quo, and focusing on future-oriented goals.

WATCH OUT FOR | Detachment from emotions, becoming overly idealistic, or losing focus due to too many ideas at once. Be cautious of resisting traditional methods simply for the sake of rebellion or avoiding personal connection in favor of intellectual pursuits.

When the moon is in Aquarius, expect an energy that encourages individuality, forward-thinking, and collaboration. This is the perfect time to step outside the box and try something new, whether in your personal life or within your community. Aquarius promotes social connection, innovation, and breaking free from outdated ways of thinking, making it a great time to focus on humanitarian projects or connect with groups that share your values.

NEW MOON IN AQUARIUS | Focus on setting intentions around innovation, personal freedom, and collective progress. Use this time to start projects that push boundaries, engage with like-minded individuals, and explore unconventional approaches to your goals.

FULL MOON IN AQUARIUS | Take a moment to celebrate what makes you unique and think about how you're making a difference in your community. It's all about appreciating your own quirks and understanding how they contribute to the bigger picture. Release thoughts that undermine your true self or your ability to connect with others.

PRACTICAL TIPS | Make small, impactful changes by swapping out your home products for more sustainable solutions, such as using reusable grocery bags, refillable containers, or eco-friendly cleaning supplies. These small shifts align with Aquarius' forward-thinking and humanitarian energy, supporting collective progress.

♓

MOON IN PISCES

BEST FOR | Deep introspection, spiritual practices, creativity, dream work, meditation, emotional healing, reading poetry, stargazing, and connecting with your intuition.

WATCH OUT FOR | Escapism, avoidance, or getting lost in daydreams and fantasies. Be cautious of overindulging in substances or distractions as a way to cope with overwhelming emotions or realities.

When the moon is in Pisces, the energy is dreamy, intuitive, and compassionate. This is a time to lean into your spiritual side, explore creative outlets, and allow yourself to rest and reflect. Pisces encourages emotional release, artistic expression, and connection with the unseen realms, making it ideal for meditation, journaling, or engaging in artistic activities that tap into your subconscious.

NEW MOON IN PISCES | It's the perfect time to heal, grow spiritually, and boost your creativity. Dive deep into your intuition, kick off a creative project, or enhance your spiritual practices. Focus on cultivating compassion, not just for others but also for yourself.

FULL MOON IN PISCES | This full moon offers a chance to close chapters that no longer serve your highest self. Engage in rituals that help you say goodbye to old patterns, embracing the wisdom gained. This is a powerful moment for seeking peace within and preparing for new beginnings with a cleansed emotional slate.

PRACTICAL TIPS | Soak up Pisces' soothing vibes with a therapeutic sea salt bath or an ocean sound meditation to calm the mind. Create a serene spa environment at home with dim lights, scented candles, and a few drops of lavender essential oil applied to your pulse points. Make sure your phone is off for total relaxation, allowing you to disconnect and recharge fully. Following your bath, wrap up in a cozy robe and further your tranquil state with a warm herbal tea to enhance the calming effects.

MOON SIGNS

UNDERSTANDING YOUR INNER SELF

While your sun sign might give a glimpse of your personality, it's just one part of a much larger astrological picture. A birth chart, also called a natal chart, which maps out the positions of the planets at your moment of birth, reveals much more, including your moon sign. This sign is considered crucial because it speaks to a deeply personal aspect of who we are, offering insights into how we respond emotionally, what gives us a sense of security, and how we intuitively care for ourselves and others.

When someone doesn't fully resonate with their sun sign descriptions, they often experience a moment of recognition once they discover their moon sign, exclaiming, "That's exactly me!" This is because the moon sign governs our inner landscape—our private emotions and hidden nature. This placement is key to understanding your inner self because it represents the part of you that operates behind the scenes—your subconscious mind and instinctual reactions. It can explain why you might find comfort in certain environments, how you express your feelings, and what you need to feel emotionally fulfilled. For instance, someone with a Taurus Moon might seek stability and enjoy sensory pleasures, while a person with a Gemini Moon might crave intellectual stimulation and social interactions to feel emotionally satisfied.

To determine your moon sign, you'll need to know the exact date, time, and location of your birth. With this information, you can use an online birth chart calculator or app to generate your birth chart. If you don't know your exact time of birth, pinpointing your moon sign can be tricky, particularly if the moon shifted signs on your birthday. You might find your moon in one of two possible signs. To narrow it down, explore the characteristics of both and see which feels more like you.

Once you know your moon sign, you can delve into its specific traits and how it interacts with other elements of your chart, offering a comprehensive view of your emotional landscape and inner needs. The following pages give a general overview of each moon sign and how they approach emotions.

ARIES MOON

With your moon in Aries, you possess a fiery, passionate emotional nature, reacting quickly and decisively. You thrive on independence and excitement, often seeking new experiences to keep your emotional life vibrant. Your emotions can be intense and impulsive, driving you to act boldly and embrace challenges head-on for emotional fulfillment.

TAURUS MOON

A Taurus Moon brings a steady, grounded approach to emotions. You find comfort in stability, routine, and sensory pleasures like good food and cozy surroundings. Your emotional well-being is deeply connected to creating a secure, nurturing environment. Patience and reliability are your strengths, providing calm and stability to those around you.

GEMINI MOON

With your moon in Gemini, your emotions are closely tied to communication and intellectual engagement. You crave variety and mental stimulation, finding emotional satisfaction through social interactions and new experiences. Your feelings are adaptable and changeable, and you thrive in dynamic, stimulating environments that keep your mind engaged.

CANCER MOON

Having a Cancer Moon means your emotions are deeply connected to home, family, and security. You have a nurturing, empathetic nature and often play the role of caregiver. Emotional fulfillment comes from creating a safe, comforting home environment and maintaining close, supportive relationships where you can retreat and recharge.

LEO MOON

A Leo Moon gives you a warm, expressive emotional nature. You seek recognition and thrive in the spotlight, finding joy in creativity and personal expression. Your emotions are linked to your sense of pride and self-worth. Emotional fulfillment comes from sharing your passions and receiving admiration and love from others.

VIRGO MOON

A moon in Virgo brings a practical, analytical approach to emotions. You find comfort in organization and routine, often seeking to improve your environment. Emotions may be reserved, but you express care through helpfulness and attention to detail. Emotional fulfillment comes from feeling useful and appreciated in a structured, orderly environment.

LIBRA MOON

With your moon in Libra, you seek harmony and balance in your emotional life. Relationships are central to your well-being, and you prioritize others' needs to maintain peace. You find comfort in companionship and beauty, striving to create harmonious environments. Emotional fulfillment comes from fostering balanced, fair relationships and environments where mutual respect is valued.

SCORPIO MOON

A moon in Scorpio brings intense, passionate emotions and a deep desire for authenticity. You experience feelings profoundly and value loyalty and trust. Your emotional life is characterized by a need for depth and meaningful connections. Emotional fulfillment comes from embracing your emotional power, facing fears, and forming profound bonds with others.

SAGITTARIUS MOON

With your moon in Sagittarius, your emotions are linked to freedom and exploration. You have an optimistic, adventurous emotional nature, seeking new experiences to keep your spirits high. You value independence and dislike feeling restricted. Emotional fulfillment comes from pursuing your passions, exploring the world, and maintaining a sense of hope.

CAPRICORN MOON

Having a Capricorn Moon means your emotions are grounded in practicality and discipline. You have a reserved, responsible emotional nature, often focusing on long-term goals and achievements. Emotional security is tied to your sense of accomplishment and stability. Fulfillment comes from achieving goals, maintaining self-discipline, and creating a structured, stable life.

AQUARIUS MOON

With your moon in Aquarius, you have an emotionally independent and innovative nature. You value intellectual stimulation and are drawn to unconventional ideas. Your emotions are often filtered through a logical lens, prioritizing the greater good over personal feelings. Emotional fulfillment comes from engaging in social causes and embracing your unique perspective.

PISCES MOON

Having your moon in Pisces brings a compassionate, dreamy emotional nature. You are deeply empathetic and intuitive, often connected to others' emotions. Your emotional life is enriched by imagination and spirituality. Emotional fulfillment comes from embracing sensitivity, connecting with your spiritual beliefs, and using your empathy to help and heal others.

SPECIAL LUNAR EVENTS

Now that you're familiar with the moon's journey through the zodiac, let's dive into some of the more special lunar events that add extra magic to the moon's cycles. Have you ever heard of a blue moon or wondered what happens during an eclipse? These rare and powerful events, along with the traditional full moons in the Old Farmer's Almanac, offer unique opportunities to harness lunar energy in new ways. Let's explore how these special occurrences can impact your practices and enhance your connection to the moon.

ECLIPSES

In astrology, eclipses are powerful cosmic events that act as catalysts for change, pushing us out of our comfort zones and revealing hidden truths. Connected to the lunar nodes—points where the moon's orbit intersects with the Earth's orbit around the sun—eclipses are linked to our soul's growth and karmic lessons. This is why they often coincide with significant life events or turning points, forcing us to confront shifts we may have been avoiding. Eclipses can feel like the universe flipping a switch, nudging us toward new directions or revealing insights that align us more closely with our true path. While these events may feel disruptive or intense, they often lead to breakthroughs that push us forward in ways we might not have expected. There are two types of eclipses in astrology: solar and lunar, each with its own distinct energy and focus.

SOLAR ECLIPSE

A solar eclipse occurs during a new moon when the moon passes between the Earth and the sun, temporarily blocking the sun's light. Think of solar eclipses as a supercharged new moon, amplifying the energy of fresh beginnings. These events can be exhilarating, marking times when big changes—like a new job, relationship, or move—feel suddenly urgent and necessary. For example, if you've been hesitating to switch careers, a solar eclipse might bring about a sudden change at work or an opportunity that pushes you to take the leap. Solar eclipses often highlight areas of your life where you need to embrace change or make a fresh start, whether you're ready for it or not. They act like a cosmic reset button, making this the ideal time to set intentions for major life shifts.

BEST PRACTICES

Take this time to set new intentions and embrace fresh starts. Journal about your long-term goals, visualize the future you want, and reflect on where you want to channel your energy. However, be cautious of acting too impulsively—solar eclipses can stir up impulsive decisions, so it's important to take time to reflect before making big moves.

LUNAR ECLIPSE

A lunar eclipse occurs during a full moon when the Earth passes between the sun and the moon, casting a shadow over the moon. Lunar eclipses mark powerful culminations and closures, often bringing unresolved emotions or hidden issues to the surface. This is the time when we're called to let go of things that no longer serve us, whether it's a relationship, a habit, or an outdated belief system. For instance, you might experience a sudden realization that it's time to release an unhealthy relationship or let go of a job that's stifling your growth. Lunar eclipses are all about release and making space for new energy, though the process can be emotionally intense. It's a time when life may force you to confront what you've been holding on to, urging you to let go so you can move forward.

BEST PRACTICES

This is the perfect time for emotional cleansing rituals, such as journaling about what you need to release or engaging in meditation practices focused on letting go. Use this energy to reflect on your inner landscape—whether it's addressing old wounds or finally releasing relationships, habits, or patterns that no longer align with your growth. Shadow work, where you confront and integrate parts of yourself you've been ignoring, is also deeply supported during a lunar eclipse.

BLUE MOON

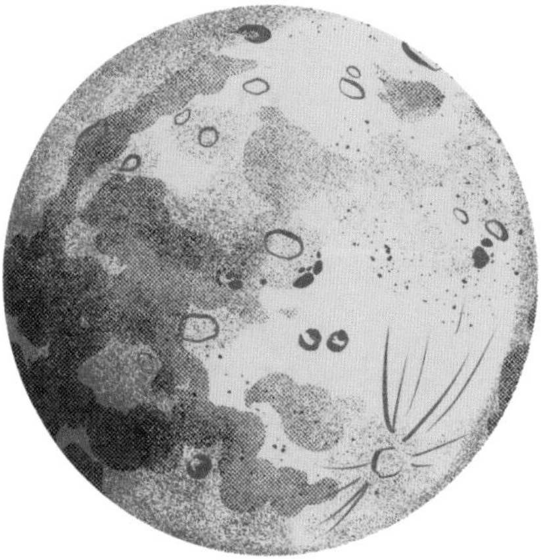

You've probably heard the term "once in a blue moon", but what does it actually mean? Surprisingly, a blue moon isn't blue—it refers to a relatively rare occurrence involving extra full moons during a specific time period, and there are three types you might encounter: seasonal, calendrical, and astrological.

SEASONAL BLUE MOON

Traditionally, this term was used to describe an extra full moon that appeared within a season. Each season typically contains three full moons, one per month. However, if a fourth full moon occurs within a season, it's known as a seasonal blue moon. This phenomenon happens roughly every two to three years.

CALENDRICAL BLUE MOON

In the past twenty-five years, the definition of a blue moon has shifted to more commonly describe the second full moon in a single calendar month. For example, if the first full moon falls on 1st October and the second on 31st October, the latter is called a calendrical blue moon. These occur about every two and a half years.

ASTROLOGICAL BLUE MOON

Lesser known, this type of blue moon refers to two full moons occurring within the same zodiac sign during one zodiac season. Like its counterparts, this happens approximately every two to three years, depending on the lunar cycle's alignment with zodiac seasons.

SO, WHY ARE BLUE MOONS SIGNIFICANT?

While calendrical blue moons might not hold special energetic significance beyond the usual full moon due to their alignment with human-made calendars, seasonal blue moons are more connected to natural cycles. However, astrological blue moons are considered particularly impactful. They occur when two full moons occur in the same zodiac sign within one zodiac season, amplifying and revisiting the themes associated with that sign. For example, imagine the sun is in Leo season. If there are two full moons in Aquarius during this period, this scenario qualifies as an astrological blue moon. In this instance, the influence of Aquarian themes like innovation, independence, and community engagement are intensified. This could mean you start Leo season by challenging your views on individuality and ending it by redefining how you connect with your community.

Here are a few practices that can help you make the most of a blue moon:

Moonlight Meditation

Sit under the moonlight, close your eyes, breathe deeply, and reflect. Let the moon illuminate your thoughts and guide you toward clarity.

Gratitude Practice

Note down three things you're grateful for this month to connect with the moon's abundant energy.

Review Themes

Think back to the start of the current zodiac season. Identify any recurring patterns and decide what needs releasing to progress.

Embrace Change

Recognize and accept transformations in your life, using this time as an opportunity for renewal and growth.

Blue moons don't come around often, but when they do, they serve as a powerful reminder that significant changes are within reach. Embrace these opportunities, and let its energy guide you towards a new chapter.

BLACK MOON

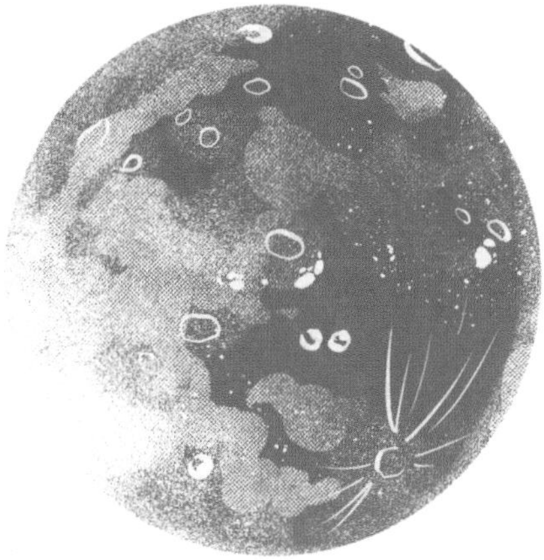

A black moon is another fascinating lunar phenomenon that occurs roughly every two to three years and appears in several forms. A calendrical black moon happens when two new moons fall within a single calendar month. A seasonal black moon arises when a season has four new moons instead of the typical three. Astrologically, a black moon occurs when two new moons land in the same zodiac sign within a single zodiac season. There's also a rarer form where February, due to its short length, experiences no new moon at all—this only happens about every nineteen years.

The black moon exudes a unique and potent energy, often heralding significant internal shifts and providing a prime opportunity for deep personal growth. This moon's dark phase fosters introspection, urging you to delve into your shadow self and discover your deepest desires and intentions. During an astrological black moon, the characteristics of the involved zodiac sign are amplified. For instance, a black moon in Aries might prompt a profound reset of your personal power and courage, pushing you to overcome old fears and embark confidently on new ventures. This doubling of new moon energy offers a chance to tackle unresolved issues and realign with the zodiac's lessons, making it an excellent time for reflection, redefining intentions, and breaking free from old cycles.

To make the most of a black moon, consider the following practices:

Shadow Work

This period is ideal for deep self-exploration. Tackle shadow work by confronting aspects of yourself that you usually ignore. Journaling your fears, insecurities, and desires can foster clarity and healing.

Let Go of the Old

The transformative energy of the black moon is perfect for letting go of outdated habits and limiting beliefs. Perform a ritual to symbolically release these burdens, like writing them on paper and safely burning it.

Meditation and Visualization

Engage in meditation to connect with the black moon's profound energy. Visualize shedding your old self and emerging renewed and empowered. This is an opportune time to realign with your highest potential and set the stage for upcoming changes.

Experiencing a black moon can be transformative. This unique phase invites you to pause, reflect on your personal journey, and initiate changes that are truly aligned with your innermost desires.

MONTHLY FULL MOONS

Did you know that each month's full moon has its own special name and meaning? These traditional full moon names come from the Old Farmer's Almanac, and they've been passed down through generations to help people stay in tune with the natural world. Rooted in a blend of Colonial American, Native American, and other North American traditions, these names were created to reflect the changing seasons and important events in the yearly cycle. From the Harvest Moon, which marks the time of year when crops are gathered, to the Wolf Moon, named for the howling of hungry wolves in midwinter, each full moon had a purpose, guiding people in their daily lives and agricultural practices.

In this section, we'll explore the meanings behind these traditional full moons, delving into their rich history and symbolism. However, it's important to remember that this system was based on observations made in a specific climate and region, so some of its themes might not fully resonate with everyone. I'll explain its limitations later on, along with a method for creating your own personalized monthly full moon names.

TRADITIONAL FULL MOON NAMES

JANUARY | Wolf Moon

The Wolf Moon is named for the howling of wolves that was often heard during the cold, long nights of January. This full moon signifies survival and endurance, making it a time to focus on inner strength, self-reflection, and the importance of community and support during challenging times.

FEBRUARY | Snow Moon

February's Snow Moon takes its name from the snowfall typical during this month. This full moon highlights themes of purification and clarity, encouraging us to cleanse our minds and spirits as we prepare for the eventual thaw of spring.

MARCH | Worm Moon

The Worm Moon is named for the earthworms that begin to appear as the ground thaws in March, signaling the start of spring. This full moon emphasizes renewal and growth, making it a time to focus on new beginnings, planting seeds for the future, and embracing the cycles of change.

APRIL | Pink Moon

The Pink Moon is named after the early blooming wildflowers, particularly the pink phlox, that appear in April. This full moon brings themes of beauty, blossoming, and awakening, encouraging us to open our hearts to new possibilities and embrace the flourishing energy of spring.

MAY | Flower Moon

The Flower Moon in May is named for the abundance of flowers that bloom during this month. It highlights themes of fertility, creativity, and celebration, making it an ideal time to focus on growth, both in nature and in our personal endeavors, as well as to appreciate the beauty around us.

JUNE | Strawberry Moon

The Strawberry Moon is named for the time of year when strawberries are ripe for picking, signaling the start of the summer harvest. This full moon emphasizes abundance, gratitude, and fulfillment, encouraging us to enjoy the fruits of our labor and share our blessings with others.

JULY | Buck Moon

July's Buck Moon is named for the time when male deer, or bucks, begin to grow their new antlers. This full moon focuses on strength, vitality, and development, making it a time to harness your power, set long-term goals, and work on personal growth and resilience.

AUGUST | Sturgeon Moon

The Sturgeon Moon is named after the sturgeon fish, which were historically most abundant during August. This full moon brings themes of abundance, perseverance, and sustenance, urging us to focus on what sustains us, both physically and spiritually, and to cultivate patience in the pursuit of our goals.

SEPTEMBER | Corn Moon (or Harvest Moon)

The Corn Moon, also known as the Harvest Moon, occurs closest to the fall equinox and is named for the time of harvesting corn and other crops. This full moon highlights themes of harvest, abundance, and preparation, encouraging us to gather our resources, celebrate our achievements, and prepare for the coming winter.

OCTOBER | Hunter's Moon

The Hunter's Moon is named for the time when game animals are fattened and ready for hunting, just before winter sets in. This full moon focuses on preparation, survival, and strategic planning, urging us to take stock of our resources, plan for the future, and ensure we are prepared for the challenges ahead.

NOVEMBER | Beaver Moon

The Beaver Moon is named for the time when beavers are most active in building their dams and preparing for winter. This full moon emphasizes hard work, perseverance, and protection, encouraging us to fortify our lives, complete unfinished tasks, and create a secure foundation for the winter months.

DECEMBER | Cold Moon

The Cold Moon is named for the long, cold nights of December as winter takes hold. This full moon highlights themes of reflection, rest, and renewal, making it a time to look back on the past year, honor the cycles of life, and prepare for the new beginnings that will come with the return of the light.

HOW TO CREATE YOUR OWN FULL MOON NAMES

While traditional full moon names carry regional significance, their relevance can vary greatly depending on where you live. These names, often inspired by North American seasonal changes and natural phenomena, might not resonate in different environments. Take February's Snow Moon, for example—its themes make sense for those living in colder climates but hold little relevance for those in tropical settings or desert ecosystems where snow is nonexistent.

Rather than sticking rigidly to these established names, why not create your own based on your local environment? This practice can deepen your connection with nature and make your lunar observations more personal and relevant. Start by exploring the flora, fauna, and seasonal events in your area. Notice how local wildlife, plants, and weather patterns evolve throughout the year, and use these observations to inspire unique full moon names that truly reflect your surroundings. You can also consider your region's cultural or historical aspects to enrich your moon-naming practice.

To provide inspiration, I've developed my own set of monthly moon names based on life in Los Angeles, California, where I live. You'll notice that there are many differences between the names I chose and the traditional ones, and that's okay—it just goes to show that you're free to choose whatever feels authentic to you and your unique environment.

JANUARY | Coyote Moon

January marks the beginning of coyote breeding season in Southern California, and their calls echo through the cool nights. The Coyote Moon honors renewal and adaptability, symbolizing the start of new cycles and the resilience needed to navigate the year ahead.

FEBRUARY | Rainstorm Moon

February often marks the peak of Southern California's rainy season. This full moon could honor the rare but nourishing rainstorms, focusing on renewal and cleansing. It teaches us to be wise with our resources and selective about the intentions we choose to water.

MARCH | Wildflower Moon

March is when the hills and valleys of Los Angeles begin to burst into color with wildflowers, like California poppies. This full moon celebrates the vibrant bloom and the awakening of the landscape, and symbolizes rebirth, fertility, and initiation.

APRIL | Chaparral Moon

The chaparral, a key plant community in Southern California, flourishes in April. This full moon reflects the tough, enduring nature of these plants (which are not only drought-tolerant but also have special adaptations to survive wildfires) that thrive in the region's unique climate, symbolizing strength and survival.

MAY | Jacaranda Moon

May is known for the stunning blooms of jacaranda trees that line the streets of Los Angeles. This full moon could represent beauty and creativity as the city transforms into a canvas of color.

JUNE | Fog Moon

June in Los Angeles is often characterized by "June Gloom", when the morning marine layer shrouds the coastline in fog. The fog dissipates as the day progresses, revealing clear skies. This moon could symbolize how clarity and understanding come with patience, reminding us that a clearer perspective is just around the corner.

JULY | Sunburst Moon

July brings the heat of summer to Los Angeles, with the sun consistently shining. The Sunburst Moon could represent vitality and abundance, urging us to harness this peak energy and put our talents on display.

AUGUST | Grape Moon

In August, grapes are harvested in Southern California's wine regions, like the nearby Santa Ynez Valley. This full moon honors the abundance of the harvest and the fruits of hard work, symbolizing celebration and gratitude.

SEPTEMBER | Ember Moon

September's dry season and wildfire risks make this full moon a symbol of release and readiness. The Ember Moon urges us to address areas of imbalance or neglect, shedding what no longer serves us to prevent future hazards and create space for renewal and growth.

OCTOBER | Wind Moon

October often brings the dry, warm Santa Ana winds to Los Angeles. The Wind Moon could represent change, transformation, and the sometimes unpredictable nature of life, reminding us to stay grounded yet flexible amidst shifting energies and committed to our goals.

NOVEMBER | Sycamore Moon

Sycamore trees, native to Los Angeles, begin to drop their large, rustling leaves in November. This full moon could symbolize transformation and release, letting go of the old to make way for the new, much like the sycamores shedding their leaves.

DECEMBER | Sunset Moon

The days are short in December, and Los Angeles experiences stunning, vibrant sunsets. The Sunset Moon could represent closure, reflection, and the beauty found in endings as the year comes to a close and we prepare for new beginnings.

CONCLUSION

Hi friend,

As you turn the final page, I hope you're leaving with a renewed sense of connection to both yourself and the magic of the moon. The practices in this book are meant to be gentle companions on your journey—there to support you whenever you need them. Remember, self-care isn't about perfection; it's about honoring where you are right now and treating yourself with the compassion you deserve. Take what resonates, let go of the rest, and trust that you are exactly where you need to be.

Lastly, if you're still reading this, thank you so much for your support. Words can't even begin to describe the depth of appreciation I have for being able to share these practices with you. It's funny—I can easily write page after page of information, but when it comes to expressing just how grateful I am, all words seem to fall short. Saying thank you can't convey how I feel in the morning, knowing that I get to wake up and do what I love every day. It can't communicate the sense of confidence I've gained through writing or encompass the boundless joy that fills me up from pursuing my dreams. All I can say is that your support has been life-changing and that I'll never take opportunities like these for granted.

Wishing you blessings and abundance,

Katie

ABOUT THE AUTHOR

Katie Huang is the founder of ***Love By Luna*** (lovebyluna.co, @lovebyluna), a leading astrological lifestyle brand, and the author of *Cosmic Self-Care*. She has written about lunar living for magazines including *Cosmopolitan*, *Teen Vogue*, and *Marie Claire*. One of her ventures, MoonBox, is a spiritual subscription box that follows the lunar cycle. She is a Pisces and lives in California, USA.

ABOUT THE ILLUSTRATOR

Amirah Sheikh is a London-based illustrator who loves using botanical and celestial imagery, earthy color palettes, and texture to create decorative and whimsical artwork. She specializes in stationery and editorial illustration, co-owning ***Lione & Sheikh***, a stationery brand where you can find her greeting cards, prints, and more.

RECOMMENDED READING

Cosmic Self-Care: Spiritual Rituals for Modern Mystics by Katie Huang (2024, Leaping Hare Press)

This book offers a deep dive into the interconnectedness of astrology, self-care, and spiritual wellness, making it a perfect companion for those looking to enhance their lunar practices. It explores tailored rituals that align with astrological events, providing readers with practical ways to harness celestial energy during different lunar phases to foster personal growth and well-being.

Moonology: Working with the Magic of Lunar Cycles by Yasmin Boland (2016, Hay House UK)

This book delves into the mystical aspect of the moon, teaching readers how to connect with its phases to optimize timing for life's decisions and activities. It covers everything from new moon wishes to full moon forgiveness rituals, making it a comprehensive guide for anyone looking to utilize lunar magic to facilitate personal transformation and manifest intentions.

Moon Spells: How to Use the Phases of the Moon to Get What You Want by Diane Ahlquist (2002, Adams Media)

This book focuses on the actionable aspect of moon magic, providing a toolkit of spells that correspond with the lunar calendar. This guide is perfect for practitioners seeking practical steps to harness specific lunar energies for casting spells that attract love, wealth, health, and protection.

MoonX App

The MoonX app is an essential tool for those practicing moon magic, offering a detailed moon phase calendar, daily astrological insights, and personalized tarot readings. It supports users in aligning their spiritual and practical activities with lunar cycles through guided meditations, holistic exercise routines, and a vibrant community platform for sharing and learning.

Quarto

First published in 2025 by Leaping Hare Press
an imprint of The Quarto Group.
One Triptych Place, London, SE1 9SH
United Kingdom
T (0)20 7700 9000
www.Quarto.com

EEA Representation, WTS Tax d.o.o., Žanova ulica 3,
4000 Kranj, Slovenia
www.wts-tax.si

A catalogue record for this book is available from the British Library.

ISBN 978-0-7112-9688-6
Ebook ISBN 978-0-7112-9689-3

10 9 8 7 6 5 4 3 2 1

Book Designer: Hanri van Wyk
Editorial Director: Jenny Barr
Commissioned by: Monica Perdoni
Senior Designer: Renata Latipova
Editor: Róisín Duffy
Senior Production Controller: Rohana Yusof

Printed in Guangdong, China TT062025

FSC
www.fsc.org
MIX
Paper | Supporting responsible forestry
FSC® C016973